Pens Down
Edited by Annabel Cook

First published in Great Britain in 2005 by:
Young Writers
Remus House
Coltsfoot Drive
Peterborough
PE2 9JX
Telephone: 01733 890066
Website: www.youngwriters.co.uk

All Rights Reserved

© Copyright Contributors 2005

SB ISBN 1 84602 192 8

Foreword

Young Writers was established in 1991 and has been passionately devoted to the promotion of reading and writing in children and young adults ever since. The quest continues today. Young Writers remains as committed to the fostering of burgeoning poetic and literary talent as ever.

This year's Young Writers competition has proven as vibrant and dynamic as ever and we are delighted to present a showcase of the best poetry from across the UK. Each poem has been carefully selected from a wealth of *Playground Poets* entries before ultimately being published in this, our thirteenth primary school poetry series.

Once again, we have been supremely impressed by the overall high quality of the entries we have received. The imagination, energy and creativity which has gone into each young writer's entry made choosing the best poems a challenging and often difficult but ultimately hugely rewarding task - the general high standard of the work submitted amply vindicating this opportunity to bring their poetry to a larger appreciative audience.

We sincerely hope you are pleased with our final selection and that you will enjoy *Playground Poets Pens Down* for many years to come.

Contents

Katerina Stamatiou (10)   1
Aidan Morrison (7)   1
Elizabeth Rushton (8)   2
Sophie Dixon (10)   3

Birchgrove Junior School, Swansea
Tom Pontin (10)   4
Dane Paterson (8)   4
Kyle Barnett (10)   5

Cliasmol Primary School, Isle of Harris
Moreen MacLennan   5
Ruaridh MacLeod   6

Dallow Primary School, Luton
Umer Salahuddin Khan (11)   6
Taslima Hussain (11)   7
Aneesa Akhtar (11)   7
Jade-Louise Baker (11)   8
Hodan Ali (10)   8
Niloy Biswas (11)   9
Abul Foyez (10)   10
Saba Nabi (11)   10
Nasir Mushtaq (11)   11

English Martyrs' Catholic Primary School, Stoke-on-Trent
Sian Hadnum (10)   11
Jennifer Cottrell (10)   12
Ellen Byrne (10)   12
Joshua Nixon (9)   13
Hannah Walachowski (11)   13
Emily O'Connor (10)   14

Glenarm College, Ilford
Labib Uddin (10)   15
Swati Thaker (11)   15
Westley Defoe (10)   16

Joanne Tien (11)	16
Branavy Irayanar (10)	17
Hussan Limbada (10)	17
Adrian Chiu (10)	18
Prené Patti (9)	18
John Burton (9)	18
Elsbeth Olaniran (9)	19
Danielle Smith (10)	19
Aadil Nawaz (10)	20
Giri Rathakrishnan (11)	21
Manhar Ghatora (10)	21
Faisal Chaudhry (10)	22
Alaina Husbands (10)	22
Mandeep Kaur Basi (11)	23
Zara Chaudhry (9)	23
Michael Kwakye (11)	24
Rachael Poluck (10)	24
Onkar Mudhar (10)	25
Vishali Ravalia (10)	25
Reshma Rajendralal (9)	26
Nedhi Vasu (10)	26

Greenacres Primary School, Tamworth
Daniel Quinn (10)	27

Groes Primary School, Margam
Liam Lovett (9)	27
Alex Hollett (9)	28
Rebecca Griffiths (9)	29
Ceejay Jones (9)	30

Hartside Primary School, Crook
Lewis Boughey (7)	30

Hayes Primary School, Paignton
Katie Hewitson (9)	31
Thomas Spicer (8)	32
Zack Jones (10)	32
Aaron Wilkins (7)	33
Kira Tapp (7)	33

Ben Hallet (8)
Harrison Fletcher (11)

Heath Primary School, Kesgrave
Jacob Steward (10) — 35
Matt Drury (10) — 35
Bill Traynor (11) — 36
James Woods (10) — 36
Joshua Gearing (11) — 37
Jessica Hollinsworth (11) — 37
Cara Warnes (10) — 38
Charlie Boon (10) — 39
Ben Emmens (10) — 40
Reece Orchard (11) — 40
Thomas Coote (11) — 41
Kelly Jeffreys (11) — 41
George Rhodes (11) — 42
Kate Edwards (10) — 42
Sofia Cucurullo-Burdett (10) — 43
Caragh McQuitty (11) — 43
Greg Pearce (10) — 44
Elena Porter (10) — 44
Fay Trenter (10) — 45
James Button (11) — 45
Ellie Pettitt (10) — 46
Shannon Timms-Mitchell (11) — 46
Tom Brelsford (11) — 47
Emma Wilkins (11) — 48
Rimini Stansfield (11) — 48
Olivia De Boise (10) — 49
Matthew Williams (11) — 50
Aidan Bobbin (10) — 50
Sarah Cubitt (11) — 51
Joe Langfield (11) — 52
Megan Whincop (10) — 53
Jessica Benneworth — 54
Abbey Burton — 54
Sian Budgen (10) — 55
Thomas Rumbellow (10) — 55
Amber Platts (10) — 56
Abi Dunnett (11) — 56

(10)	57
lin (10)	58
(10)	58
w (11)	59
ər	59
yshire (11)	60
nally (11)	60

Herington House School, Brentwood
Alice Gough (10)	61
Holly Stringer (10)	61
Emma Lander (9)	62
Lucy Rogoff (10)	63
Charlie Whittaker (9)	64
Stephen Massey (9)	65
Finella Waddilove (9)	66
Charlotte Henderson (9)	66
Sagana Sivakumaran (10)	67
Alice Church (9)	68
Alex Burns (9)	69
Thomas Morey (9)	70
Jessica Tuck (9)	71
Zainab Khatib (9)	72

High March School, Beaconsfield
Hannah Manning (9)	72
Giulia Gibbons (9)	73
Isabel Spoerry (8)	73
Grace Brazier (9)	73
Francesca Leonard (9)	74
Ella Smart (9)	74
Sophie Palmer (9)	75
Katy Hills (9)	75
Timona Chetty (9)	76
Isobel McVey (9)	76
Emily Stephens (8)	76
Claire Read (9)	77
Francesca White (10)	77
Sophie Lomas (10)	77
Georgia Hurrell (9)	78
Elena Monks (8)	78

Annabel Johnstone (9)	79
Jessica Kinsey (10)	79
Rosanna Sasson (10)	80
Celine Bautista (10)	80
Lucy Stephens (10)	81
Isabel Hutchings (10)	81
Cristina Hall (10)	82
Katie Hyde-Coppock (10)	82
Georgina Taylor (10)	83
Julia Clarke (10)	83
Annabelle Hussey (9)	83
Joanna Jones (9)	84
Chloe Coutts (10)	84
Bethaney Morrison (10)	85
Isobel Kynoch (9)	85
Sarah Aspland (9)	86
Judy Marsden (10)	86
Emily Burnett (9)	87
Emma Curley (10)	87
Dara Cormican (10)	88
Anushka Mehta (8)	88
Charlotte Hurley (9)	89
Taylor Dangerfield (9)	89

Hywel Dda Junior School, Cardiff

Tyler Jay Andrews (11)	90
Cameron Smart (10)	90
Class 7 & 8	91
Chelsea Fenn (10)	91
Ben Moore (9)	92
Dyllon Thomas (9)	92
Gemma Wozencroft (10)	93
Dominy Hale (9)	93
Sheekilah Jones (10)	94
Jessica Jones (8)	94
James Coles-Bessant (10)	95
Jordanne Wilson (9)	95
Charlotte Devine (11)	96
Lucy Macnamara (8)	96
Katie Pounds (11)	97
Lauren Price (10)	97

Emma Laver (10)	98
Jessica Thomas (9)	98
Gabrielle Evans (10)	99
Joseph Connolly (9)	99
Jade Edmunds (11)	100
Charlotte Friis (9)	100
Anthony Somersall (11)	101
Bethan Sterio (9)	101
Paige Chick (11)	102
Laura Griffiths (9)	102
Chelsea Bedford (11)	103
Amy Jones (11)	103
Joshua Parsons (11)	104
Kim Powell	104
Leanne Stimpson (11)	105
Leanne Browning (11)	105
Emma Russell (10)	106
Jason O'Brien (10)	106
Gabrielle Newing (11)	107
Ffiôn Bisatt (9)	107
Christina Mitchell (11)	108
Hayley Prowse (11)	109
Shane Pritchard (11)	110
Stephanie Truman (11)	111
Sophie Newsham (11)	112
Ciera Honey (11)	113

Iona Primary School, Argyll
Euan McIntyre (11)	114

Ledbury Primary School, Ledbury
Laura Channing (11)	114

Longdon St Mary's CE (VA) Primary School, Tewkesbury
Daisy Yeates (10)	115
Rosie Woodward (10)	115
Charlotte Webber (11)	116
Guy Vickery (10)	116
Isabella Thompson (10)	117
Sophia Franklin (10)	117

Laura Scott (11) 118
Jaimie Sinclair (10) 119
Christian Cox (10) 120
Jack Larner (10) 120
Carianne Martin (11) 121
Harvey Carter (9) 121
Victoria Houghton (10) 122
Samuel Carter (9) 122
Holly Barrett (10) 123
Alice Kerrigan (10) 124
Harriet Harker (10) 125
Lizzie Fletcher (10) 126
Danielle Price (10) 127
Ryan Jones (11) 128

Middleton Primary School, Wollaton Park
Naylor Chambers (10) 128
Megan Richmond (10) 129
Bryce-Lucas Scalia (10) 129
Clare Saxton (10) 130
Beth Marsden (9) 130
Jasmine Shearsmith (10) 131
Aerran Dirs (10) 131
Jack Brown (10) 132
Mehreen Khan (9) 132
Katie Kinnear (10) 133
Isobel Upjohn (9) 134
Charlotte O'Leary (9) 135
Suleman Shamshad (9) 136

Mill Lane Primary School, Chinnor
WIlllam Moody (10) 136
Hannah Harvey (9) 137
Sophie Greenwood (9) 137
Adam MacKerron (9) 138
Samantha Bull (9) 130
Connor Wheeler (10) 139
Peter Cooper (9) 139
Vicky Price (10) 140
Ellen Higgs (10) 140
Lucie Brand (10) 141

Lauren Bishop (10)	141
Abbie Bratt (10)	142
Nicola Lawrence (9)	143

Oakfield Primary School, Totton
Sophie Diaper (10)	144

Old Fletton Primary School, Peterborough
Isobel Thompson (8)	144
Shona Barrett (9)	145
Finola Murtagh (8)	145
Jordan Heather (8)	145
Natasha Petchey (9)	146

Peartree Primary School, Welwyn Garden City
Hanna-Joe Cox (7)	146
Yilmaz Taycur (8)	146

Peniel CP School, Carmarthen
George Williams (9)	147
Llywela Davies (10)	147
Dafydd Jones (10)	148
Matthew Edward Kilgariff (11)	148
Bethan Cumber (9)	149
Claudia Jones (9)	150
Amelia Cox (10)	150
Robert Jones (10)	151

Portway Junior School, Andover
Tammie Leigh Sinnott (9)	151
Ben Biddlecombe (9)	151
Georgie Wheldon (9)	152
Elle-Louise Heard (9)	152
Jack Short (8)	152
Eleanor Roche (9)	153
Flinn Kenward (8)	153
Laura Jones (8)	154
Daniel Andrews (8)	154
Matthew Jenkins (9)	154
Adam North (8)	155

Abigail Portsmouth (8)	155
Chloe Rowland (8)	156
Sam Beecroft (10)	156
Jamie Barry (9)	156
Jessica Allmark (9)	157

St Edmund's CE Primary School, Mansfield Woodhouse

Natasha Byrne (11)	157
Kelly Burbanks (11)	158
Kelsay Higton (10)	158
Stacey Redfern (10)	159
Brooke Jephson (10)	159
Sorel O'Berg (10)	160
Martin North (10)	160
Anthony Glynne-Jones (10)	161
Ethan Brown (10)	161
Tia Read (10)	162
Alice Sentance (10)	162
Coral Booth (10)	163
Emily Minett (10)	163
Chelsey Nicholls (10)	164
Billy Simpkin (10)	164
Chloe Seddon (8)	165
Kristian Pye (11)	165
Natalie Mauri (11)	166
Jessica Beresford (10)	166
Kia Martin (10)	167
Kristie Richardson (10)	167
Joshua Wardle (10)	168
Rebecca Lounds (9)	168
Zak Wycherley (9)	169
Sophie Mason (8)	169
Ben Jones (9)	170
Jade Clay (10)	170
Stacey Hill (10)	171
Ashley McMillan (9)	171
April Shannon (9)	172
Chloe Jevons (9)	172
Michael Wallis (9)	173
Adam Gallagher (9)	173
Annabelle Cassidy (10)	174

Daniel Hardwick (9)	174
Lewis Jephson (9)	175
Katie Rose (10)	175
Ricky Blakey (9)	176

St James' CE (Aided) Junior School, Derby
Leanne Greasley (9)	176
Tanzeela Hanif (9)	177
Attiyah Riaz (8)	177
Somera Hussain (9)	178
Miriam Khan (9)	178
Gwyneth Mabo (9)	179

St Patrick's RC Primary School, Grangetown
Nazneen Bamji (11)	179
Niall Boyce (11)	180
Dionne Scarico (10)	180
Chloe Pride (11)	181
Kirsty Nash (11)	181
Michael Harrington (11)	182
Lauren Green (10)	182
Hannah Phillips (10)	183
Shanice Nicholls (11)	183
Rachael Fanning (10)	184

St Peter & St Paul Primary School, Bexhill-on-Sea
Jessica Elliott (11)	184

Sandon JMI School, Buntingford
Callum Thomas (9)	185
Paige Strong (7)	185
Luke Geaves (8)	186
Grace Gumble (8)	186
Hal Jones (8)	186
Hannah Stout (9)	187
Jake Long (8)	187
Connor D'Arcy (8)	187
James Tucker (9)	188
Amelia White (8)	188
Danielle Moon (7)	188

Josh Volpe (8)	189
Matthew Tucker (8)	189
Robert Potts (8)	189
Faye Piggott (7)	190
Philippa Watkins (7)	190
Kristie Childs (8)	190
Matthew Stout (8)	191
Daniel Morris (7)	191

Shapinsay Primary School, Orkney

Andrew Marwick (9)	191
Gail Zawadski (8)	192
Rachel Muir (8)	192
Jake Houston (8)	192
Emily Farquharson (11)	193

Siddington CE Primary School, Siddington

Taylor Wall (9)	193
Sam Burgess (10)	193
Sapphire Rogers (10)	194
Emma Walker (9)	194
Oberon Rogers (10)	194
Daniella Keen (10)	195

Westbury-on-Trym CE Primary School, Bristol

Harry Tainton (10)	195
Charlotte Vincent (11)	196
Danielle Johns (8)	196
Emier Villanueva (10)	197
Chloe Paddock (8)	197
Daniel Squire (11)	198
Mathilda Forrester (9)	199
Megan Dymmock-Morgan (7)	199
Carys Gilbert (8)	200
Demi Orchard (11)	201
Jenny Seaborne (10)	202
Sophie Haydon (7)	203
Katy Farmer (10)	203
Nisha Dave (8)	204
Bláithín Garrad (8)	204

Jack Hooper (8)   205

Ystruth Primary School, Blaina
Jade Legge (11)   205
Abbie James (10)   205
Corey Williams (10)   206
Tanith Parfitt (10)   206
Beckie Price (11)   206
Gemma Ball (11)   207
Daniel Wall (11)   207
Adam Hughes (10)   207
Rhys Watkins (11)   208
Demi Cooper (11)   208
Aimee Smith-Holden (10)   208
Ieuan Ward (11)   209

The Poems

Books

Books, a vehicle to escape reality.
a source of transportation to a different world,
a time machine to another era;
a trip to impossible worlds
that only imagination can complete.
The anticipation of turning the page,
joining the characters' feelings and adventures,
seeing what they see,
doing what they do,
following their every footstep in their imaginary worlds.
I open the book, my eyes glued to the page . . .
as if in a trance by its magical powers, gaining my interest,
as I read phrases, sentences, paragraphs, pages, chapters,
all so real, lively and engaging.
I complete all my duties in a haste,
as if no time to waste,
to get to my book; as if in a race.
And now, I'm curled up in my bed, my thirst quenched.
A book is a treasure . . . and a treasure it shall always remain.

Katerina Stamatiou (10)

Volcanoes

Rocks on fire,
Thick black smoke,
A tall black mountain,
Red-hot lava.

The rough surface of the stone,
The ground shaking,
Tha lava burning,
The heat blazing.

The fire crackling,
The rocks crashing,
The lava bubbling,
The ground trembling.

Aidan Morrison (7)

When Granny Was Eight

When Granny was eight,
Her mother laid a plate,
Of delicious mince pies,
And hid them from the eyes
Of Granny and her sisters,
Altogether three great tricksters.

But the key to the cupboard they did find,
And creeping up the stairs they climbed,
Then they thought *oh just for fun,*
What's the harm in taking one?
But they ate, and ate, and ate
So that they left only eight.
And quite soon there was only one,
After that they left just *none!*

But then Christmas came,
And they all took the blame.
And Mother screamed and yelled and shouted,
For how the naughty girls had flouted.
Oh how the girls cried!
And then Mother sighed,
But the girls could not eat the new pies that she baked,
For they all found their stomachs ached!

Elizabeth Rushton (8)

The A - Z Poem

A ges and ages it takes in a year.
B edtime is boring when there's nothing to do.
C ats are very cute when they don't scratch.
D ad is a good drummer, a noisy drummer!
E ggs come from chickens, the same as a bird.
F airies are one of my favourite things.
G uitar I play, it's nice and calm.
H ospitals is where I don't like going because it makes me sad for the sick people.
I like football, PE and literacy.
J ingle bells, jingle bells, Batman smells Robin laid an egg!
K ind, my friends are kind except one.
L ilac, pink, purple, blue and green are my favourite colours.
M illennium is a long time, a millennium is a 1,000 years.
N ice to have a friend who's side by side with you!
O ctober the 14th is my birthday.
P ine cones come from fir trees.
Q ueens are beautiful, some are ugly.
R abbits are bouncy, so are rubber balls.
S limy snakes, slimy snails and shiny stars!
T igger is bouncy because of his tail.
U niverse is bigger than the Earth, moon and galaxy.
V enice is a country that lives on water.
W hen something is over it's impossible to forget.
X mas is what I don't say and Christmas is what I do.
Y asmis is a Brat doll, my favourite Brat doll!
Z ebras are my sister's favourite animal for the sake of stripes.

Sophie Dixon (10)

The Power Of Words

Words can
Haunt or help,
Destroy or rebuild,
That is the power of words.

Words are the foundation,
Societies and creation.
There are famous words that have been said
By the living and the dead.
They are respectfully remembered
But they are just . . . words.

Sticks and stones break your bones
But . . . they mend.
It's words that hurt or soothe your feelings;
They are always remembered,
Those little, lingering . . . words.

Tom Pontin (10)
Birchgrove Junior School, Swansea

The Power Of Words

Words can be eternal,
They can take you to paradise,
They can take you on a roller coaster ride,
They are unseen power,
They are strong as a heart.

Words can be devastating,
They can be as poisonous as venom,
They can be chaotic,
They can be extreme.

Words are gentle,
They can be soft as a polar bear's fur,
They can be as gentle as water,
They can be soft as air,
My favourite word is eternal.

Dane Paterson (8)
Birchgrove Junior School, Swansea

The Power Of Words

The power of words will stand in my heart,
Will always follow me wherever I go,
Throughout my life they will start to grow.

Some of these words in my heart are kind and small,
But others are big and nasty
Like a big cold stick.

Kyle Barnett (10)
Birchgrove Junior School, Swansea

Colours

Why is the sky blue?
Why are clouds white?
Why is the sun yellow
And why is the grass green?
Why is the sea the same colour as the sky? Why? Why? Why?
Why are clothes different colours? Why? Why? Why?
Why are hills brown and green?
Why are lions yellow and black?
Just one thing! Why? Why? Why?
Why are elephants grey
And why are cats all sorts of colours? Why? Why? Why?
Why are sheepdogs always black and white?
Why are windows clear?
Why are treetops green
And why are their trunks brown? Why? Why? Why?
Why are white boards white
And why are sheep sometimes black and white?
Why are crabs red? Why? Why? Why?
Why are books all sorts of colours? Why? Why? Why?

Moreen MacLennan
Cliasmol Primary School, Isle of Harris

My Dog

I once had a dog,
His name was Bob.
He was black, white and tan,
Fast as a cheetah
And as high as a small van.
As long as a mini bus
And as wise as an owl,
He followed me everywhere
Except from school.
He was 14 years old, 8ft tall
And 7ft long!
He was the funniest dog in Amhuinnsuidhe
And the fastest too!

That's my dog!

Ruaridh MacLeod
Cliasmol Primary School, Isle of Harris

Angel Of War

The carpet made by soldiers is getting redder every second.
Individuals killing their wills and spilling their blood like water.
The wallpaper of the trenches is made by blood
Yet there is still 10,000,000 gallons left.
The blood creeping,
Filling every corner of the room with despair.
Bombs giving no rest, screeching every second,
Killing humans like ants.
The cry of the soldiers dying a horrendous death.
Soldiers afraid to touch the butt of the rifle.
Soldiers opposing their thoughts and feelings.
The natural sensitivity of human beings dripping away.
Only one colour which is in sight, *dark red!*

Umer Salahuddin Khan (11)
Dallow Primary School, Luton

If I Was A Teacher . . .

If I was a teacher,
My pupils would work all day.
If I was a teacher,
My pupils would have no play.
If I was a teacher,
I would shout and scream.
If I was a teacher,
I would be nasty and mean.
If my pupils didn't listen I'd make them run,
I would even do it for some fun.
I would be like Cruella - evil and bad,
I'd make the children cry and be sad.
I'd punish them for the smallest things,
I'd punish them for wearing rings.
But to think of the marking, piles and piles,
It would make me run a mile.
To think of all the shouting my neck would go sore,
All that explaining would be a right bore.
So I think it's best if I stay a student
And you stay a teacher.

Taslima Hussain (11)
Dallow Primary School, Luton

Fat Kids

Kids screaming in my face,
Shouting only what they can see,
But they don't know the real me.
They always poke me,
Sitting alone, silence hurts,
They say fat kids will never be free.
Kids crowd around,
Girls skip around me,
Fat kids treated like trees.

Aneesa Akhtar (11)
Dallow Primary School, Luton

Owls

Three mice scuttering across the ground
Like they are running away from something.
Three pure white mice.

Leaves fall from trees like parachutes
Gliding softly in the air,
Then getting pushed away by the wind.

Three mice are squeaking loudly
As if they are having a slow and painful death
Or have been injured.

Rustle of leaves get louder and louder
As if people are stamping on them.
Owls from across the road call for help and warning.

Hard branches are under my feet with broken twigs everywhere.
I get in my warm home, leaves squelch under my feet like wet mud.
Happiness fills me from top to claw as my heart beats louder.

Jade-Louise Baker (11)
Dallow Primary School, Luton

Park

Us,
You and me,
Let's play on the swing,
Enjoying the day in the park,
We're winning against the strong wind,
Chasing the rustling leaves, what fun that is!
We're winning against the strong wind.
Enjoying the day in the park,
Let's play on the swing,
You and me,
Us.

Hodan Ali (10)
Dallow Primary School, Luton

Lost . . .

The sky was a sparkling velvet,
Covering everything in sight.
The vivid moon shone brightly
Reflecting its magical light
On the bottomless lake;
Shining like diamonds.
The gnarled and wrinkled branches of the tree
Reaching out for me as I run breathlessly.
I was like a moving bird,
Imprisoned in a cage.
All I could hear was my heartbeat,
My blood running to my head
And my almost noiseless footsteps.
The trees spy me suspiciously as I
Gradually enter their territory.
Suddenly, something moves,
Footsteps, slowly coming towards me.
An icy chill creeps down my spine,
I feel cold blood run swiftly through my veins.
I am petrified,
Just truly petrified.
I try to run,
But my legs are rigid as stone,
I cannot move a single bone.
Without a warning,
A voice speaks.
The words will haunt me for the rest of my life,
If I live much longer.

'Your death is not far from you . . .'

Niloy Biswas (11)
Dallow Primary School, Luton

School Emotions

Children are working on poems to impress me with what they can do.
The beautiful wavy, green trees are exuberant.
Next door's children are shouting and crying as loud as a lion roaring.
Children are shouting and screaming at me as if they are mad.
The pencil cases are praying for a child to open them.
The pencils are screeching as the books are quickly talking.
Home time arrives and children are happy but chairs are crying.
Parents worried so heavily if their children don't arrive.
The children have gone home and made me happy after
                                                    the hullabaloo.

Abul Foyez (10)
Dallow Primary School, Luton

Death

Happiness all over the world, especially this little girl
Playing with her friends in the garden but she doesn't know
When the clock strikes midnight
She will not be here tomorrow,
Because she is going to die
And this is not a lie.
Hearing the laughter of pain and death laughing away to kill.
That's a knife to everyone who live and die.
Hearing the rain crying away, crying down to Earth
But that little girl just doesn't know what's going on,
So she just carries on,
But then she felt it between her heart.
She just went inside and cried till her heart sank,
Now that girl is just sitting and writing this poem,
Because that girl is *me*.

Saba Nabi (11)
Dallow Primary School, Luton

Fear

Fear is scary,
It sounds like footsteps in my attic,
It feels like being killed,
It smells like dead people's blood,
It tastes like eating spiders,
It reminds me of the vampire.

Nasir Mushtaq (11)
Dallow Primary School, Luton

Frog's First Goal

I've seen rabbits, giraffes, cats, bats, dogs
But never frogs.
He's very small, not very tall
And even mistaken for the ball.
The players came out, (a stampede he thought
With all the bangs, booms and roars).
He got kicked in a puddle at the back of the net,
While the crowd cheered, he was soaking wet.

At the end of the match
While everyone clapped,
The frog gets attacked
And gets hurt!
He hops off, sad
While the crowd goes mad,
That the team has won once more,
Once more, as they did before,
But this time the poor frog
Got mistaken for the ball!

Sian Hadnum (10)
English Martyrs' Catholic Primary School, Stoke-on-Trent

My Two Chinchillas

My chinchillas like to squeak,
They really are active, but you have to peek.
When you walk in the room they stare at you,
And when you're away they like to chew.
They munch all day on their treats and snacks,
Their big wire tails swish behind their backs.

If you make them angry they may just bite,
I think they like to eat Marmite.
One is grey and one is black,
When they eat they have a snack attack!
You see, my chinchillas are the best,
They are called Bubbles and Squeak.
Our house is their nest.

Jennifer Cottrell (10)
English Martyrs' Catholic Primary School, Stoke-on-Trent

Little Folk

Fairies flutter in the air,
They have magic fairy dust.
The fairy face, it is so fair,
Making people happy, they must.

Leprechauns are small in size,
Pots full of gold,
Pure mischief in the eyes,
Don't stop when they are told.

Pixies sit on toadstools
Making mischief fun.
Under there is nice and cool,
Oh, no! Look what they've done!

Gnomes sit catching fish
In gardens or in parks.
I bet sometimes they wish
That they could sing like larks.

Ellen Byrne (10)
English Martyrs' Catholic Primary School, Stoke-on-Trent

World Cup Celebration

Come on England, we're on your side,
We're all supporters, full of pride.
We'll all march with you on the way up
And watch with glee when you lift the Cup.

Owen, Beckham, do not fear,
You will fill us full of cheer,
When you take us to the top
Celebrations will not stop.

Joshua Nixon (9)
English Martyrs' Catholic Primary School, Stoke-on-Trent

Orang-Utans

Orang-utans, orang-utans
Live in trees.
Orang-utans, orang-utans
Pick each others fleas.

Orang-utans, orang-utans
Eat bananas.
Orang-utans, orang-utans
I don't think they like koalas.

Orang-utans, orang-utans
They look very cute.
Orang-utans, orang-utans
Especially in a furry suit.

Orang-utans, orang-utans
They don't make a peep.
Orang-utans, orang-utans
Sssh! They're all asleep.

Hannah Walachowski (11)
English Martyrs' Catholic Primary School, Stoke-on-Trent

My Midnight Enchantment

One cold and wintry midnight,
Guess what I saw?
Some marvellous things
Like unicorn wings
And a dinosaur standing tall.

But not just that,
I saw a Cheshire cat
And a cheeky little dog.
They were dancing around,
Making not a sound,
When someone began to sing.

We all wondered what it was,
At least I did.
Then out of the sky
Came a beautiful cloud of fairies!
They enchanted us
And made us want to sing.

The dinosaur sang
With the most amazing voice
Which was worth listening to,
But, unfortunately, I was sent to bed
Because my mum was coming soon.

I just had time to slip into bed
As she whispered, 'Goodnight.'
But I knew it was not just to me,
It was also to my friends of the night.

Emily O'Connor (10)
English Martyrs' Catholic Primary School, Stoke-on-Trent

Darkness

The church struck a ghostly twelve o'clock
And ghosts strike free from the crooked church,
Skeletons emerge from their ghostly graves,
Horses huddle near the warm hay,
While phantoms hover across the street,
Haunting every house.

The spirit haunts my house at night,
In the gloomy hours, it scares me.
The dark ghoul floats around the living room
And gives me a great fright
And the storm keeps me awake.

Labib Uddin (10)
Glenarm College, Ilford

Goldfish And Broomsticks

Swimming like fast little sharks,
The goldfish explore a new home
And like to see it in the dark.

They find it so amazing
They don't stop gazing
Around my lovely room.
They look at my Hoover
And think it's a witch's broom.

Scared they hide in their houses
And peek out every minute to see
If the broom is gone.

When satisfied they glide out
To hear a peculiar strumming
And find it to be a weird din
And go to hide
Because of my voice.

Swali Thaker (11)
Glenarm College, Ilford

Frost

A soft glittery blanket
Covers the sleeping cars
While the early morning
Dew dangles from the
Emerald green shoots
That have emerged
From the compact
Loam soil.

Its cold bitter taste
Glides along my
Soft, flexible tongue.
I step out,
The frost has gone,
The cars stand shivering
In the freezing cold.

Westley Defoe (10)
Glenarm College, Ilford

Nature's Wonders

I collect nuts,
I collect worms,
I collect all sorts of things,
I can fly high in the air,
I can run like a cheetah,
I can wriggle about,
I can go under the soil
To sniff for intruders.

I can be sneaky,
I can scratch my enemies,
Lie in all day,
Feeling the warmth in my body,
Tasting the rain in the air,
Smelling the wild berries,
Hearing the trill of the world.

Joanne Tien (11)
Glenarm College, Ilford

The Green Eyes Of Jealousy

Like a sour lime in my mouth,
My insides quaking with fury,
Only inflaming the hot-headed.
How it awakes the hot-headed devil within me,
Taking over my body,
Uncontrollably, my feelings submerge me,
I am reborn a monster of jealousy.

A precarious volcano waiting to erupt,
Hot lava gushing in torrents.
Great waves of destruction crashing together,
Boiling liquids churn the depths of my subconscious.
An irritation, an aggravation. 'Unfair!' you say to yourself.
The green poisonous flicker of my envy flames burns my interior.
I still live, fiend of jealousy.

I feel trapped, bound by my scalding envy,
Envy that bubbles continuously within me,
My thoughts and feelings focused on wrong emotions.
My teeth grind, seething,
My wrath simmering, saliva frothing,
I cower in the monstrous shadow.
But I won't let it conquer me,
I will conquer the ogre of jealousy.

Branavy Irayanar (10)
Glenarm College, Ilford

Alone

You're the one who broke up my friends,
The boy who turned away.
You're the one who decided to bully,
To beat me up that day.
You were alone,
But I'm the one who brought you back,
Who made you friendly and nice.

Hussan Limbada (10)
Glenarm College, Ilford

Angry Teacher

Red head, exploding volcano and cutting blade.
His face was like a streaming kettle,
The eyes were pools of lead
And his moustache was taking a flight to another person
And his chin was as sharp as his tongue.
His mouth was spitting saliva like a violent storm at sea
And his voice was as loud as a tiger.

Adrian Chiu (10)
Glenarm College, Ilford

Anger

Boiling rage
Building up, wanting to be free.
My red-hot face
Exploding like a volcano.
Inside I feel my blood bubbling up.
I'm being dragged across jagged rocks,
Red hot chillies scorch my mouth.

Prené Patti (9)
Glenarm College, Ilford

Angry You

When you are angry you have grinding teeth,
You see exploding volcanoes and thunderstorms,
Your face turns red,
Eyes are watering,
You hear bombs exploding and creatures roaring.

John Burton (9)
Glenarm College, Ilford

Tiger In The Jungle

Softly touching the warm ground
Of each and every paw,
The king of the jungle finally reaches
The grassy land
And finds its prey,
Gently pounces and the rodent makes a move
And walks to find another rabbit.

Darkness hits the jungle,
King of the forest has a great zebra,
He tries to find his way home
To feed the king and find shelter,
The zebra lies flat on the floor dead,
Another tiger walks closer to him and they share,
Together they go to sleep,
Together they find morning,
Parrots flutter, monkeys leap, snakes slide,
This is the jungle.

Elsbeth Olaniran (9)
Glenarm College, Ilford

Wind

A slight of wind
Blows me away.

Bumping into lamp posts,
Slapping me.

Whipping me, battering me.
I'm walking my way
Through the shivering cold,
A mile away from home.

Danielle Smith (10)
Glenarm College, Ilford

The Alarm Clock

Ring-a-ding-ding,
I rub my eyes and look around,
What I can't figure out is what makes that sound,
I turn my head, see the alarm clock on the floor,
I pick it up and read the time,
I can't believe it's nearly nine!
I get out of bed and put on my uniform.

Beep! Beep!
It's my mum!
Oh I wish I could run,
Because she is here to spoil my fun,
She takes me in the car,
Before I could plead,
She had gone too far.

Ding-a-ling-ding,
The school bell rings and I drop everything!
I don't know what class I am in,
I know I've got to pay attention,
Or I will get detention.

Bleep!
With one eye on the clock,
Every minute seems like an hour,
Home time approaches,
Outside I can see cars and coaches,
As it gets to half-past three, we are going to be free!

Aadil Nawaz (10)
Glenarm College, Ilford

Darkness

A portal to death,
A realm of loneliness,
A key to all secrets,
A lock to bright light.

An odour of rotten blood,
An aroma of witches' perfume
And the smell of cold breeze.

It tastes like salty venom,
Fire sears on your tongue,
Devil's breath asphyxiates.

The end of time
Like evil is near
And you can confront your fear.

The creaking of a door,
The rattling of a window,
The sigh of the wind
And snoring and sniffling.

Giri Rathakrishnan (11)
Glenarm College, Ilford

Leopard

Gentle hunter,
His tail plays on the ground
While he crushes the skull.

Beautiful death
Who puts on a spotted robe
When he goes to his victim.

Playful killer
Whose loving embrace
Splits the antelope's heart.

Manhar Ghatora (10)
Glenarm College, Ilford

Swans

With a long clean neck
Pecking at food,
Slowly moving,
Warning everybody with their quacks,
As clear as a sheet of paper,
Seen from miles out,
Cygnets poke their heads out of their brittle white shells
Touching the shell it cracks.
With necks like giraffes they are swans.

Faisal Chaudhry (10)
Glenarm College, Ilford

Nature

It takes its course wildly,
Roaming around contentedly.
Bugs and plants socialise
And together skip the streets merrily.

Roses and tulips twist and turn,
Their vines and leaves clash.
This is how nature communicates,
In the most unbelievable way.

Life has this miracle,
Which it takes for granted.
Insects and flowers go back home,
For another night of peaceful rest.

The world plays minute games,
In which nature can enjoy.
Trees sway in the gentle breeze,
While squirrels gather nuts to take home.

Alaina Husbands (10)
Glenarm College, Ilford

Fear

As I was sitting on the park bench,
My fear had awoken me,
The black spirit was standing by my frayed shoes.

His frothy spit glided over my face,
As he spoke of evil,
He dismantled my smile and shook my nerves.

My heart was beating itself up inside me,
It felt like a wet dagger being thrown into my guts.

Suddenly, a white door loomed right in front of me,
I limped through,
I walked on, numb, it went on like a boring campfire song.

When I opened the sixth door,
My family were staring at me,
Merry and warm like the flower-patterned duvet the hospital nurse
                                              had given me.
All the fear ran away like scared mice.

Mandeep Kaur Basi (11)
Glenarm College, Ilford

The Eye In The Keyhole

Like a glittering owl's eye,
It worries me a lot.
Whenever I call my mum,
The gleaming orb disappears.
My sister thinks I am crazy,
But I just trust myself.
Its sharp eyes glow at me.
I spend my days looking at it
And it spends its days looking at me.

Zara Chaudhry (9)
Glenarm College, Ilford

Nature

I look all around
And see nature,
Its smell is of a perfume
And smiles like a baby.

Its eyes gaze at me,
As if I am up to mischief,
But all I am doing is,
Giving it a helping hand from its troubles with man.

The birds' cuckoo is music to my ears
And the rustling river is that of a crowd rejoicing,
The flowers dance gaily in the wind
And the sun's rays put a smile on my face.

But unfortunately we are destroying nature,
The thing we all need to survive,
And very soon,
This beauty will be gone.

Michael Kwakye (11)
Glenarm College, Ilford

Butterflies

Butterflies are like a soft pool of pillow in the cloud,
They flutter in the soft blows of the wind.
They have a soft touch
Like feathers from white doves of Heaven.
And a single plume fills the love
In people's hearts.
Butterflies have wings like banana leaves.

Rachael Poluck (10)
Glenarm College, Ilford

Jealousy

Green the sea of envy,
Is this me? I think to myself.
Has a monster been subdued inside of me?
Forcing me to dislike the ones I love,
And unite with the ones I dislike.
Changing me for the ages,
Letting the evil spirit of jealousy take over my soul.

Onkar Mudhar (10)
Glenarm College, Ilford

My Imaginary Friend And I

In the shining twilight,
My imaginary friend and I,
Walked around the
Grassy hillside,
Amazed by what we saw.

In the glowing moonlight,
There we saw the foxes dancing
And the ducks quacking.
The man in the middle with the drums
And guitar.

In the bright light,
We stood there in silence,
Then looked at each other,
With faces as white as a ghost,
In amazement.

In the shimmering stars,
My imaginary friend and I,
Walked round the
Grassy hillside,
Amazed by what we saw.

Vishali Ravalia (10)
Glenarm College, Ilford

Jealousy

He is a green-eyed monster who burns inside you,
He is like a bottle of dangerous acid waiting to be thrown upon
his victim,
You can never see him but you can feel him inside you tickling.
'He's got more money, she's got a better car,'
Those are the chants that bring him to life.
Everybody hates him being with them.

Reshma Rajendralal (9)
Glenarm College, Ilford

Again And Again

Feeling so dull and numb,
Nothing whatever to do,
I feel awful for what I did to my friend,
I will never do it again.

I feel my heart has been ripped up,
Yet was so excited to showing her what I had got,
I had embarrassed so badly,
She never wanted to see me again.

Sitting all alone in the corner,
Looking like a black sun,
Seeing birds which had trouble to fly,
Over again and again.

I hear a plop joining the ocean of tears,
Getting higher and higher - minute by minute,
Telling ways of being her friend but
Refusing again and again.

With her around everything tasted
Like a coffee with extra sugar,
Without her it felt like hot chocolate without any powder in it.

Nedhi Vasu (10)
Glenarm College, Ilford

Winter Breeze

Look at the bare trees in the icy wind
Encircling a desolate playground,
Around the edge emerald icicles,
White frozen ivy climbs like spiders,
Conifers surviving until the summer sun.

Clouds that look like fleecy animals,
Skylarks calling in the sky,
Little ponds that look like seas,
Chains that look like webs gleaming in the twilight.

Daniel Quinn (10)
Greenacres Primary School, Tamworth

School Day

I like school, I think it's fun,
It's time to learn and not time to run.
Maths is cool but Welsh is glum,
Sir is cool until you run.

Playtime is good to laugh and play,
Football is the name of the game we play.
Hockey is rubbish, I don't like to play,
But it's better than writing any day.

Drawing and games are exciting to play,
Until it's too loud and the teachers complain.
Then time for silence and exercise books,
The teachers change into grumpy spooks.

We have assembly every day,
Where Mr Saunders has lots to say.
I fidget, talk, move and sway
Hoping the end is on its way.

When school days are over and done
It's time to have lots of fun.
Can't wait for the end of the day to come,
As everyone loves to see their mum.

Liam Lovett (9)
Groes Primary School, Margam

Our School

Of all the schools I would like to be,
Groes Primary is the place for me.
That is where I go every week day,
Whatever the weather I'm on my way.

By nine o'clock the school bell goes,
There at the door our headteacher shows.
In a line we wait and stand,
For our teacher to give her command.

When in the classroom we all sit down,
I think my teacher deserves a crown.
If you want to write just go and look,
For a pencil or paper, or maybe a book.

But writing graffiti? Don't be a fool,
Creating an eyesore is really uncool.
I love Man U or David luvs Lily,
Means your a vandal and makes you look silly.

There in the playground I like to be,
That's where all the children all run free.
I really do think my school is so great,
That's where I go to meet my mates.

The cooks are there to give us our dinner,
The meals are great, we're onto a winner.
In school I'm reminded of my family,
The safe environment is the place to be.

The cleaners are working ever so hard,
The dinner ladies watch us out in the yard.
Then if I fall or scrape my knee,
I get sent to our lovely secretary.

So in all respect where credit's due,
All school staff deserves a medal, every one of you.

Alex Hollett (9)
Groes Primary School, Margam

Friendship

I walk to school each day,
My mum waves goodbye,
My friends meet me at the gate,
At least the weather's dry.

The bell goes and we line up,
This happens every morning,
The teacher starts to laugh at us,
As most of us are yawning.

We all work hard at school,
There's so much to do,
We read and write all morning,
Then paint all afternoon.

The bell sounds, it's playtime,
We all rush out to play,
The girls go off together,
It's our favourite time of day.

We all have skipping ropes,
To play a counting game,
But one girl trips as she skips,
And we have to start again.

The boys play football in the yard,
Tom goes to get the ball,
The boys shout, 'Can you climb?'
They've kicked it over the wall.

It's the end of the school day,
The clock reads half past three,
I wave goodbye to my friends,
I'm home in time for tea.

Rebecca Griffiths (9)
Groes Primary School, Margam

Playtime At The Park

Standing in the playground,
Making lots of noise,
Watching all the children
Playing with their toys.

We swing on the swings,
We swing so high,
When I look up,
I can reach the sky.

We head for the slide,
With a big long drop,
And when I look up,
I'm far from the top.

We run to the see-saw,
My friend and I,
We sit at each end
And watch the others go by.

We go to the climbing frame,
We twist and bend,
I've had so much fun today,
I wish it would never end.

Ceejay Jones (9)
Groes Primary School, Margam

River Nile

The Nile is blue
So are the boats.
The sun is orange
So is the sunrise.
Sun is a shadow
On the Nile
Boats are sailing.

Lewis Boughey (7)
Hartside Primary School, Crook

Alien Invasion

What's that noise I hear?
It's coming from outside,
Tiptoe, tiptoe, very quietly,
As quiet as can be.

It's in the garden,
It's huge, it's massive,
It's gathering quite a crowd,
It's dreadfully noisy.

To hold you from suspense, my friends,
I really must include,
This huge, this massive thing,
Is a *space saucer* in the sky.

Don't scream, don't shout, my friends,
You will scare it away,
This space saucer with colourful lights,
Is nothing but a fake.

But just then -
Oh dear, how awful -
It seemed to come alive,
Out they came and took us by surprise.

Let's chase them down the aisle,
Let's get them back to the home planet,
They're more scared of us infact,
Scared of us in their ball game hats.

At last, oh great! We've got them trapped,
Push them, push them in,
Start it up,
Oh dear, oh no, Tom's inside that saucer!

A long way to space above the clouds,
So have you got your clothes and shoes?
I sure hope so, you'll be there for long,
I hope you come back someday
To see your friends and home!

Katie Hewitson (9)
Hayes Primary School, Paignton

Family

You can call on your family - they're always there
The love you give them is beyond compare.
When you're down in the dumps
They'll be there to cheer you up.
They will help you on your way
They make your tears go away.
When I am sad
They'll be there to make me laugh.
When I can't do stuff
They'll be there to lift me up.
I don't know what I would do
Without my family to see me through.
If I didn't have a family seeing me through
I don't know what I would do.
Your family are special people
Who help you on your way
They make your spirits rise
Each and every day.
My family is great
I say it every day.

Thomas Spicer (8)
Hayes Primary School, Paignton

Tsunami Disaster

We were all horrified
At the sights of the tsunami disaster
Thousands were left homeless
Tears were shed
And houses were destroyed
But hope wasn't lost
No one gave up
In the tsunami disaster.

Zack Jones (10)
Hayes Primary School, Paignton

Friends

Friends, friends, they help you when you're hurt
They help you when you're stuck at work
Friends play with you
They sit next to you in class
So you should be friends
My friends look out for me
So every friend should have a friend as well
If it was like that for everyone
Life would be so happy
Friends help you when you're lonely
They help you when you are sad
So do all of these things.

Aaron Wilkins (7)
Hayes Primary School, Paignton

The Playground

People jumping,
People skipping
Boys kicking a ball.
Simon stop!
Kirsty don't!

Children crying,
Children happy
Teachers all around.
I hate you! That's not nice!
Let's go and play with the ball.
That's nice.
The playground is full of people.
Everybody loves to go to the playground.

Kira Tapp (7)
Hayes Primary School, Paignton

Hard Homework

Homework, homework, homework
Homework every day.
I just can't stand it
It's just always homework
Spelling tests
All of it
It's all too much to handle
Get it away
Get it away
It's all homework every day
Homework all night
I'm not the only one who gets it all
Everyone gets it
We can't stand it
No one can handle it
It's homework every day
Homework, homework, homework
Hard spelling tests
So it's homework
Just homework every day
Homework all day, all night, all evening
And it's too much!

Ben Hallet (8)
Hayes Primary School, Paignton

The Train Station

Memories of the old, abandoned station
Still lurk in the vandalised walls.
The wooden railway sleepers
Lie on the hard, cold stones,
Worn down from years of screeching brakes
And driving sleet.
The station still lives on.

Harrison Fletcher (11)
Hayes Primary School, Paignton

Electronics

TV has been made to watch
It's been made for us to have something to do.
The Hoover has made it easy for us to clean
It has been made for us not to do it by hand.
The telephone is useful
Because we don't have to go and see the person for real,
We just talk to them on the telephone.

All of these have been made for us,
To make life easier so we don't have to do much,
Just get in touch or switch it on
And get an icon on the computer if you have done something wrong.
Don't get angry, be strong, pick up the phone,
Call an engineer to fix it.

But you don't have to be a scientist to do so
Or Homer Simpson, if you have got it wrong say, 'Doh!'
Just use this modern technology to help us.
Don't get upset that we haven't got enough technology,
Or have a bet on who is going to be the first person
                              to make some more.
Just be thankful for what we have got.

Jacob Steward (10)
Heath Primary School, Kesgrave

Monkey

Monkey, monkey where are you?
In the jungle?
No, in the zoo.
You long to be free,
Swinging from a tree,
Playing with your friends,
Until the day ends,
But you're stuck in the zoo,
With nothing to do,
Just looking at people,
Looking at you.

Matt Drury (10)
Heath Primary School, Kesgrave

Rallying

You don't know where you're going,
You have to trust the person sitting next to you,
You have to put your daring, sacred life on the line,
Hope that he doesn't read one word wrong,
If he did make that grave mistake,
The consequences would be fatal.

But once you know where you're going,
And you trust the person sitting next to you,
You can release the raging devil inside,
Use the devil to accelerate mind bogglingly fast,
Use him to reach supersonic top speeds
With his everlasting evil power,
Generated from your ferocious engine.

But when the devil inside is high in Heaven
His evilness will give you . . .

Bill Traynor (11)
Heath Primary School, Kesgrave

Think

Think, think,
Think of the people
Lots of people,
Think of the people who died.
One month has gone past,
We don't know if it will last.
There's not many people alive.
When it happened the people who were surfing
Now had to dive,
Now it's all over,
People are giving food from above,
Help the people
Don't just stand there,
Do something.

James Woods (10)
Heath Primary School, Kesgrave

All Alone

Alone and hungry in the streets
In the alley it reeks
In the alley I want to eat
I walked out and I got a beating
It was cold everywhere
And after long I could not bare
I'm really hungry and I need to be fed
I look like I'm going to be dead
All the other kids are lucky
I'm alone and hungry in the streets
I don't want to be near any other kids.

Joshua Gearing (11)
Heath Primary School, Kesgrave

Street Child

He was near death's door
Then a man found him on the floor.
He had ear problems and mumps
But he took him from the dumps.
The man gave him a bed
Until he was fully fed.
When he went to sleep
He never made a peep.

He became rich,
He found him in a ditch.
He taught and told
Until he grew old.
Unfortunately one day
He passed away.
He wishes he was here,
But he has no fear
Because he knows he's in his dreams.

Jessica Hollinsworth (11)
Heath Primary School, Kesgrave

Lonely Caterpillar

Once I saw a caterpillar,
Squirming on the ground,
He was squirming down the garden,
He was squirming all around.

When I picked the creature up,
He looked really sad,
When I went to put him down,
He made me feel rather bad.

When I looked once again,
A bird was in the sky,
I had to run away with him,
I couldn't let him die.

I ran straight down the garden,
I ran straight down the road,
And as I kept on running,
We saw a little toad.

We followed our new slimy friend,
To a place so calm,
But when we looked upon the grass,
We saw a caterpillar farm.

I put him down with his friends,
And he seemed to smile at me,
Then I just left him there,
Because I knew how safe he'd be.

Cara Warnes (10)
Heath Primary School, Kesgrave

Street Child

I am alone on the street,
With nothing to eat.
Nothing is clean
And everyone is mean.
Every man that walks by,
I give a great sigh
And wish I had help.
In hope one day,
A man would say,
'Come with me and you will see,
That you are loved.'

And then one day,
A man came my way.
That man said,
'Come with me and you will see
That you are loved.'
So off we went,
In the pouring snow,
And sang 'a tallyho'
Until I was fed
And I went to bed.
I combed my hair
And said a prayer,
'Thank You Lord,
Thank You Lord.'

Charlie Boon (10)
Heath Primary School, Kesgrave

Football

The match must start,
The mascots depart,
The goalkeeper dives,
A defender slides,
An attacker scores,
And gets a deafening applause,
The ref gives a red card,
Number 9 takes it hard,
The teams carry on,
For the match is not won,
Half-time is here,
The fans have a beer,
The players are hyped up,
They want the golden cup,
Another goal has been scored,
The raving crowd roared,
The whistle is blown,
Time to go home.

Ben Emmens (10)
Heath Primary School, Kesgrave

Tsunami

I saw a wave, it got bigger and faster,
I started to run as fast as I could,
The wave hit the land,
I grabbed a tree for my life.
The wave made me let go,
I got washed to the other side of town,
All of the houses were washed away,
About one hour later it stopped,
I couldn't see anything,
Everything was gone,
It's tragic.

Reece Orchard (11)
Heath Primary School, Kesgrave

Poor Child

The child is ill, his name is Bill
He's lonely and bony.
His hungry and starving
He's sick, tired and bare.
But then along came a man called Dr Barnardo
And he picked him up and changed his life.
Now he's safe and loved,
He's not hungry or lonely or bony.
He's clean and he's not embarrassed to be seen.
People respect him and they don't kick him or pick on him
But the main thing is his saviour,
Barnardo is his hero.

Thomas Coote (11)
Heath Primary School, Kesgrave

The Secret Animal

The silent footsteps by the tree,
That only sometimes people see.
They're big and so is their tail,
They'll leave a trail
Of footsteps that can come to you.

They hunt at night,
When it's not light,
In search of prey for their tea.
They'll start to lick,
They can break a stick,
You will find them in cages near you.

They'll stare at you,
And you'll stare at them,
At the golden and black stripes they have.
They're all alike,
You'll have a fright if you don't like . . .

Tigers!

Kelly Jeffreys (11)
Heath Primary School, Kesgrave

Street Child

Alone and wet,money I seek,
Alone as I moan, sitting infested and infected.
As people walk by, alone I cry.
I walk around, going past all playgrounds,
As I see birds go by, slowly I die.
I see a swan, alone and warm,
As I take on mould, suddenly I turn cold
A man comes and picks me up
And my life has come again
I see some meat and I bare to eat.
Now I write with ted and now I go to bed.

George Rhodes (11)
Heath Primary School, Kesgrave

Victorian Street Child

When I got thrown out of my house,
There weren't very many tears,
To be honest I think they wanted me gone,
But I didn't have any fears,
After a few days though
I grew cold, hungry and weak,
I was filthy and damp in that dump,
It was dark and very bleak,
But I got found by Doctor Barnardo,
He was very nice and took me in,
I had a home and I felt safe,
I was no longer thin,
I felt loved and clean,
I was so very glad,
For I feel if I had been left alone,
I would have been driven mad.

I love this new life of mine!
It's better than living on the streets.

Kate Edwards (10)
Heath Primary School, Kesgrave

Street Child

I was starving and cold,
Then my clothes turned to mould,
I was frightened and upset,
When it rained I got wet,
I was tired and terrified,
I was frozen and petrified,
I wanted to go home,
So I would not be alone.

Sofia Cucurullo-Burdett (10)
Heath Primary School, Kesgrave

Street Child

I'm filthy, dirty
Cold and lonely
No one is here beside me.

My mum threw me out
Because I was not working
Hard at the factory.

Now I'm hungry
Searching for scraps of food.

I feel unwanted
I'm crying because no one is there
I'm dying, please somebody help me

Today my life got better
I'm not filthy or lonely
I feel wanted, people are around me
I feel so thankful
Because I have been helped.

Caragh McQuitty (11)
Heath Primary School, Kesgrave

Street Children

The horrible, cold streets infect my body,
I can hardly find a scrap of food,
There is nothing to wash in
Apart from the sewage running down the street,
Lots of us are sick and ill, dying every day,
I hear something coming, it is a man,
He pulls me up, he says he's going to help me,
He takes me back to his home and cleans me up
And looks after me forever on.

Greg Pearce (10)
Heath Primary School, Kesgrave

Holiday With You

It's fun to go on holiday
Once in a while
You could go abroad,
To where the sun is warm and glowing
Or maybe you could go
To a place that's always cold and snowing.

You could go to France
And climb the Eiffel Tower
Perhaps to Italy
And the Leaning Tower of Pisa
Or maybe even Egypt
To see the Sphinx of Giza.

But best of all I like to swim
In water clear and blue
To jump and splash and just have fun
On holiday with you.

Elena Porter (10)
Heath Primary School, Kesgrave

Street Child

I was cold, in pain and lonely,
I was on my own, I didn't feel wanted,
I was ragged and starving, nobody loved me,
I was ever so dirty and smelly
Everyone looked but just walked off,
There were flies buzzing round my head
And I smelt of dirty food.

Today my dream came true,
I was really excited
I felt safe, wanted and finally loved.
I was thankful the people were kind,
They fed and washed me
And I smelt fresh!

Fay Trenter (10)
Heath Primary School, Kesgrave

All Alone On The Streets

It's cold and dark, you can't see anything.
You don't know what to do.
You are sleeping on the floor with rags.
People are looking at you as if you do not count.
Feeling hungry because you have no food.
Feeling thirsty because you have not had a drop to drink.

Home sweet home!
Now feeling warm and lots of light.
Now my eyes are so bright I can take in every sight.
My comfy bed so warm and nice.
No one staring at me while I sleep.
People now think I count.
Breakfast, dinner and tea, that will do for me.

James Button (11)
Heath Primary School, Kesgrave

Three O'Clock Friday

Three o'clock Friday I'm home at last,
I can now forget the week that's passed.
They took my snack on Monday in break
And replaced it with a disgusting fake.
On Tuesday in class they took my book
And gave me an unpleasant dirty look.
In lunch on Wednesday they took my food,
Which left me in an angry mood.
On Thursday they called me names and started teasing,
But I couldn't really hear because I kept on sneezing.
Today their leader was not there,
So bully me they did not dare!
But it's 3 o'clock so at last I am free
And for the whole weekend they can't get at me.

Ellie Pettitt (10)
Heath Primary School, Kesgrave

Your Feelings

We each have feelings, me and you,
Sometimes happy, sometimes blue.

Feeling happy, feeling sad,
Feeling really, really bad.

Afraid I feel when I get curious,
But sometimes I can get very furious.

Feeling lonely when there's nothing to do,
Feeling hungry when there's nothing to chew.

We all feel excited when we make friends,
But I'm so sorry this poem has to end.

Shannon Timms-Mitchell (11)
Heath Primary School, Kesgrave

The Food Fight

He comes to the dinner hall with his dinner,
Not noticing the banana skin
And he slips!
And drops the dinner on someone's head -
Nice shot!

The mucky person fights back,
But he misses the guilty man -
The crowd boos and shouts.

Five minutes later, the whole dinner hall joins in
And food hits the girls, the boys, the dinner ladies,
Even the headmistress!
Whoever threw that is going to have a year's worth of detention!

It is complete chaos in the dinner hall,
Just look at it now,
All the teachers are involved now,
And just think - this all started from a banana skin!

Food on the floor, tables, walls,
Dinner ladies, teachers,
Little kids crying,
Waiting to come into the hall.

Ten minutes later, the bell rings,
Stops the food fight of a lifetime,
Everyone's annoyed that the chaos has come to an end
And it's back to class!

Tom Brelsford (11)
Heath Primary School, Kesgrave

Tigers

Tigers are orange, black and white
Plus they are such a great sight.
Nothing beats watching them run
As they race about in the burning sun.
They soon walk over to the water hole
Puffing and panting like a troll
Sometimes you're lucky enough to see them kill
It feels like you've dry-swallowed a big pill.
They will outrun you any day
And if you mess with them you will pay.
Don't get dragged towards them by their piercing eyes
Otherwise you will be waving all of your goodbyes.

Emma Wilkins (11)
Heath Primary School, Kesgrave

In The Car

We are goin' on holiday.
Me and my best friend.
Wake up at 6am,
Pack up all make-up.
Off we go down the road
Stoppin' off at McDonald's
For a greasy breakfast.
Mum getting really annoying
Because of toilet stops.
Little bro really annoying,
Finally get there.
Week goes too quick
It begins all over again.

Rimini Stansfield (11)
Heath Primary School, Kesgrave

The Solar System

The sun is a burning ball of fire,
To give us all light, on every single planet
My very easy method just speed up naming planets.

Mercury has a dark blue colour
And its core is made of iron
Mercury is closest to the sun.

Venus is a fiery orange
With lots of lightning flashes
And blazing temperature.

Earth is blue in colour
With swirling clouds and fresh green land
Never stops spinning on its axis.

Mars is deep red
It looks like a rusty desert
But very cold in temperature.

Jupiter is the biggest planet,
With its orange and white stripes
And its marvellous 'red storm',

Saturn is orange,
Which is made of liquid secured by gravity
And its seven cold rings.

Uranus is an outer planet
With ten vertically rotating rings
It is covered with a dense fog.

Neptune is dark blue
With its many clouds
And its 'great dark spot'.

Pluto is light blue,
It is absolutely tiny
And it is extremely cold.

Olivia De Boise (10)
Heath Primary School, Kesgrave

The Big Game

We are running on the field
Last week's injuries have healed,
We win the toss,
This won't be a loss,
The game is underway,
We are keeping them at bay.
Racing, running,
We can hear them coming.
They have good skill,
But it's still nil-nil.
We run with the ball,
They trip us, we fall.
We get a free kick,
I take it quick.
We have a shot,
The ref points at the centre spot.
We win the game,
We are all in immense pain.

Matthew Williams (11)
Heath Primary School, Kesgrave

Football

Football's the best, football's great,
Anyone can play no matter what colour or race,
You need to work in a team
And it doesn't matter if you end up unclean.
I love playing football, it's always on my mind
And so fantastic the feeling it gives me inside.

Aidan Bobbin (10)
Heath Primary School, Kesgrave

Summertime

It's summertime so let's all shout,
Have a laugh and mess about
Go to the beach and swim in the sea
Or have a picnic with biscuits and tea

Wear all those dresses that you've never worn
Or climb up trees and get them torn
Play in the park and have some fun
Or go for a walk in the blinding sun

Summertime, the best in the year
No rain, no bad weather, not even a tear
Go on an outing or have a holiday,
'What a season,' we all say.

See all the sunflowers growing high
When the days are longer than night
Go out and have fun with all your mates
Be little devils or be little saints.

Have a barbie, get the family around
Eating and drinking and sitting on the ground
Burgers and hot dogs and drinking Coke
Laughing and joking with all the folk.

Bike rides down a country lane
Hear birds sing their sweet refrain
Play in the park till it gets late
Hide 'n' seek and skip and skate

Summertime what can I say
I wish it never went away
Dance about, sing and cheer
Aren't we glad when it is here.

Sarah Cubitt (11)
Heath Primary School, Kesgrave

Championship

Two thousand and five
Will this year be the year?
Not just to survive
To go up with no fear.

Will Wigan go up?
I see no reason
As long as they're behind us
At the end of the season.

What about West Ham?
They beat us at home.
They've managed to get
Some good players on loan.

Sunderland FC
A north-eastern team
Are yet to come down here
Our *victory* will be seen.

Just in the play-offs
Preston North End
They have some good players
But drive me round the bend

We can't forget Sheffield
If you want my advice
They can't be that good
We have beaten them twice.

Derby have our old boss
Burley is his name
At Pride Park it was 3-2
That won't happen again!

A 1-1 draw with Reading
Both goals at the end
We need not worry for QPR
They simply can't defend

There is nobody left to worry us
If you look at the rest
To stop our dream of going up
And being one of the *best*

Come on Ipswich!

Joe Langfield (11)
Heath Primary School, Kesgrave

Summer Loving

Summer's just around the bend,
I hear drummers drumming,
Spring's nearly gone,
Looking into the night sky,
See the sky, tell me summer's about to come,
I can't wait for the new day.

Hot air is steaming,
Right beneath my feet,
Summer's here, it's not going away,
Life's changing forever,
Life's hotter than a rainbow,
Why can't life stay like this?

As summer's coming to an end,
Hot beaches become cold again!

Winter, autumn, summer, spring,
Are all nice seasons of the year,
With Christmas in December,
Guy Fawkes in autumn,
Lambing in spring,
Wimbledon in summer,
And all other kinds of sports.

Megan Whincop (10)
Heath Primary School, Kesgrave

Goal!

The whistle blows, the game has started,
The football teams shook hands and darted,
Everyone stands and shouts in the crowd,
And the referee started to shout, *'It's a foul!'*
Rooney took over and went for the ball,
The crowd went wild and suddenly, *'Goal!'*
So it's one-nil to England, *'Way to go!'*
The crowd settled down and watched the show,
Bad luck to England, Spain have scored,
While the English crowd booed, the Spanish crowd roared!
But now it's half-time we've drawn on this round,
Now let's hope England will win and be crowned,
We're off to get hot dog and chips,
Hopefully we'll win the championships!

Jessica Benneworth
Heath Primary School, Kesgrave

Victorian Children
(Dedicated to Doctor Barnardo, the first man to build a home for orphans)

Here I stand cold and alone,
Nowhere to run, no place called home
Blank walls on a dusty street,
Dirty hands and mucky feet
Loneliness should turn to hope
But I'm climbing a never-ending rope
People passing who seem visible
But I feel like I'm invisible
They don't even stop to take a look
They just turn me over like a page in a book
There I stood cold and alone
But now I've got somewhere to run called home
My tattered clothes will go to waste
For now I can taste the victory of being safe.

Abbey Burton
Heath Primary School, Kesgrave

Summer

Summer is the sunny season,
For laughing, playing and having fun.
Summer's when you go and stay,
Somewhere nice on holiday.
You can go swimming or to the beach,
Or go in your own private swimming pool.

Summer's the time when the sun is high,
And there are hardly any clouds in the light-blue sky.
When thunderstorms strike in the warm black night
And the rain comes down in little showers,
It's nice and hot but there's not much shade
But going swimming would cool you down!

Sian Budgen (10)
Heath Primary School, Kesgrave

Football, Football, Football

It is all I want to do,
With my head up high in the sky,
Running madly to shoot
The other players say, 'Man that's frightening,'
To see me running down the wing like lightning.
I stop and spin as the adrenaline runs through me,
Then blast a shot as hard as Rooney.
The keeper dives as far as he can get
But seconds later the ball flies into the net,
That shot it went just like a missile,
Then the ref blew the full-time whistle,
My teammates ran and lifted me up,
Oh my God, we've won the cup!

Thomas Rumbellow (10)
Heath Primary School, Kesgrave

Foggy Nights

Foggy nights start to show,
And all the people know,
Winter comes with cold noses and ears,
While all the people have no fears.
No children on the slide,
Because it's nice and warm inside.
Wellie boots and bobble hats,
Headlights like eyes of cats,
Moonlight shines in the dark,
All around dogs bark.
Grass crunches underfoot,
I can only hear, I cannot look
Because . . .
Eyes have no sight,
On this dark foggy night.

Amber Platts (10)
Heath Primary School, Kesgrave

Snickers

S is for squeaking, Snickers never stops!
N is for nibbling, when Snickers has his food!
I is for intelligent, something Snickers is not!
C is for cuddling, something Snickers loves!
K is for kindness, something Snickers always shares!
E is for entertaining, Snickers always makes me laugh!
R is for rummaging, something Snickers always dares!
S is for Snickers, my most favourite guinea pig!

Abi Dunnett (11)
Heath Primary School, Kesgrave

Victorian Poem

I live on the streets in the city,
The darkness, the coldness, the pity
Sometimes I wonder,
In rain and the thunder,
Why I am thought of as less.

People walk down the streets without caring,
But when they are further they're staring,
I think I am bad,
I'm lonely and sad,
In these poor streets of London.

I live on the streets in the city,
The darkness, the coldness, the pity
Sometimes I wonder,
In rain and the thunder,
Why I am thought of as less.

I smell and I'm in tats
The constant screeching of rats,
I know I'm unwell,
Only time will tell,
Whilst I live in these conditions.

I live on the streets in the city,
The darkness, the coldness, the pity
Sometimes I wonder,
In rain and the thunder,
Why I am thought of as less.

I wish the people would help me,
But poverty will never set you free,
The way we are treated,
Money won't meet it,
We'll suffer and die in despair.

Gabby Lake (10)
Heath Primary School, Kesgrave

Trampolining

I like trampolining, because it is really fun,
I have a coach and friends from trampolining.
Sometimes you can bounce really high or really low.
On a trampoline you can do anything
Like a twist or a front drop and tuck jump.
That's why trampolining is my best subject in the world.

Lauren Laughlin (10)
Heath Primary School, Kesgrave

Cars, Cars, Cars

Cars are good
Cars are fast
Most cars are built to last.
Some cars are nice
Some are ugly
Some are like the Trotters' car
Lovely jubbly.
Red, black, yellow,
Any sort of shades
All sorts of sizes can be made.
From limousines
To Mini Coopers
From monster trucks
To space troopers.
Every country has its car
Germany, England, even USSR.
Prices vary, cheap or dear
Automatics or ones with gears.

So what is your favourite car?

Jack Bartram (10)
Heath Primary School, Kesgrave

Ice Queen

In the freezing cold world,
It's summer but too cold
The ice queen is plotting an evil plan,
No one can stop her, no man.
It's the ice queen,
She is really mean,
She likes the cold,
That's what was told.
It's like a fantasy without meaning,
There are ice doors sealing,
You would recognise it from a scene,
That's the story of the ice queen.

Ryan Sparrow (11)
Heath Primary School, Kesgrave

Candy Land

Yummy, yummy, in my tummy,
Sweets for children, Daddy and Mummy.
Creamy ones and many more!
Sweets and candy that I adore!
Red and green laces,
That get stuck to your faces!
Yummy in my tummy!
Sweets for children, Daddy and Mummy.
Jelly eggs,
Sherbet legs,
Black tangy liquorice
A candy land for me! I wish!
Yummy, yummy in my tummy,
Sweets for children, Daddy and Mummy!

Sheree Driver
Heath Primary School, Kesgrave

My Two Favourite Seasons

Autumn
As conkers start to fall to the ground,
I have ten that I have found.
The leaves on the ground start to rustle,
Busy people start to bustle.
The leaves turn brown and yellow,
The wind's so bad you have to bellow.

Summer
When children go to buy a lolly,
Seems like summer makes them jolly.
In the morning out pops the sun,
Mums over do it with the suncream, seems like a tonne.
It takes longer to grow dark,
So you have more time at the park.

Daniel Darbyshire (11)
Heath Primary School, Kesgrave

The One Ring

The one Ring is great and powerful
And better than the rest
Made by the Lord Sauron.

One must take the one Ring
Back to the fire of Mount Doom
Where it was made.

The power of the Ring must be unmade
Only the great evil must be undone
This the price that must be paid.

There is no other way,
There is no other choice
Only one must take it in.

Gavin MacInally (11)
Heath Primary School, Kesgrave

Violet Flowers

Out of all the rainbow's vibrant hues,
Violet brings the sweetest news.
Violet is a shy little flower,
Which may have grown in a bright red bower.
Deadly nightshade's a poisonous plant,
Don't be deceived by the pleading chant.
Lavender smells so fresh and sweet,
A few drops on your pillow is a real treat.

The lovely buddleia, butterfly bush,
Make sure you don't disturb the butterflies sshh!
The foxglove stands so tall and straight,
Whatever you do don't be its playmate.
The colours of the garden bring such a pleasure,
The memories of summer are something to treasure.

Alice Gough (10)
Herington House School, Brentwood

Blue Belle

The blue of her eyes,
Matches the skies.
The ocean deep
Cannot compete.
Her little blue frock
And her tiny pale socks
Make her outfit complete.
Her lovely long hair
Is golden and fair
She is the same age as me
And she always will be.
She is special to me,
As you can tell
My beautiful porcelain Blue Belle.

Holly Stringer (10)
Herington House School, Brentwood

What Is Red?

Red is an apple,
Red is a cherry,
Red is a rose,
And a ripe strawberry.

Red is ruby on the stars,
Red is for faraway Mars,
Red is for red wine,
Red is for danger - so stop in time!

The fireman's red hat,
Is too big for my head,
So I wear a red bucket,
When playing instead.

Red is a postbox,
Where letters go,
Red is for pain
And a throbbing toe.

Red is for sweet lips,
Ready to kiss you,
Red is for a cold nose,
And flushed cheeks too.

A heart is red on playing cards
It is also your chest.
Red is the colour
That I like best.

Emma Lander (9)
Herington House School, Brentwood

Green Is . . .

Green is a hot pepper
Burning your tongue
Fresh juicy grapes
Sitting in the sun.

Green speckled frogs
Jumping around,
While the grass in the meadow
Moves without a sound.

The Emerald City
All shiny and bright
The eyes of a cat
As they catch the light.

The face of a witch
All haggard and scary
The fur of the *Grinch*
All smelly and hairy.

The skin of a dragon
All covered in scales
The lively lizard
With a long pointed tail.

Rosemary, parsley, coriander
And thyme
Growing so neatly
All in a line.

The colour of envy
A poison within
Which is why it is one
Of God's deadly sins.

Lucy Rogoff (10)
Herington House School, Brentwood

What Is Red?

Red are the cherries that grow on the trees,
Red is the blood when I graze my poor knees.
Red is the engine that puts out the fire,
Red is the heart that is filled with desire.

Red is the ruby that flashes on gold,
Red are the fingers that freeze with the cold.
Red is the postbox that carries my letter,
Red is the colour of my favourite sweater.

Red is the wine that passes my lips,
Red are the roses and red are the hips
That follow the blooms in the autumn so red,
Red are the dahlias that grow in the bed.
Red are the leaves as the year fades away,
Red is the sky at the end of the day.

Red are the peppers and red are strawberries,
Red are tomatoes and all kinds of berries.
Red is the sweetness of cherries and apples,
Wrought by the sun that through leaves gently dapples.

Red can be many things, most of them nice,
But what else can it be, now let me think twice.

Red is my face when covered in shame,
Red is my face when taking the blame.
Red is my face after running a mile,
Red is my face when I try not to smile.

Red is a show-off, there's no doubt about it,
But one thing I know - we just can't live without it.

Charlie Whittaker (9)
Herington House School, Brentwood

Red Is . . .

Red is blood,
Red is fury,
Red is the anger running through my veins,
It is evil running through my blood.

Red is a warning,
Red is danger,
Red is the fire and the fire engine putting out the flames.

Red is wine,
As we dine,
Red is roses and rubies that I must give to my sweetest valentine.

In a cosy cottage
At the edge of a meadow
I slumber in my bed and smell the scent of roses in the spring air.

Red is apples,
Red is strawberries with cream
That you eat on Wimbledon Green.

Red is the berries I love to eat,
Juicy and sweet,
Red is pies and crumbles baking in the oven.

Red is for the Arsenal,
The Gunners, or so they say,
But I'm a Tottenham fan, through and through.

So out with the red and in with the blue.

Stephen Massey (9)
Herington House School, Brentwood

Red

Red is the best colour in the world,
Strawberries are red so they are my favourite fruit.
Even my unfashionable mother wears a red suit
It is her favourite colour too.
It runs in my family because
My older sister Poppy adores the colour red.
It's even the colour of the flower in her name
And by the way, she's insane.
My dog is a bit overfed
He is supposed to bark *woof-woof*
But instead he barks *red-red*
My other sister is mad about
The fashion label Red Or Dead,
'I've never heard of them,' I said.
So you see I cannot live without the colour red,
It's the last thing I think about before I go to bed.

Finella Waddilove (9)
Herington House School, Brentwood

What Is Red?

Red is a tomato juicy and round,
Red is a rose beautiful and pretty,
Red is a ruby sparkling through the rock,
Red are our lips so we can eat and drink,
Red is our blood when we graze our knees,
Red are our cheeks when we are embarrassed and want to hide.
Red are strawberries and raspberries with cream,
Red is an apple when we eat it to the core,
Red is a sun setting for the night,
Red is a fire engine which rescue people from fire.
Red is a postbox when we post letters.
Red is wine when we drink and laugh.
How could we live without the colour red?

Charlotte Henderson (9)
Herington House School, Brentwood

The Meaning Of Red

Red is just like a bright red heart,
And which tastes like an apple tart.
Red lipstick on your lip,
A bit darker on the tip,
Red is for the lovely roses,
In their beautiful positions and poses,
Red is famous for the bird robin,
Sometimes you get red on your chin.
The lights are shining bright red,
As the traffic goes when we are in bed.
Red as houses and the bricks,
Time goes by as the clock ticks.
Red means to be good and take some care,
Or sometimes to be aware,
Red is a ripened strawberry,
And by that fruit we will be merry.
The postbox with its super red,
'I've got a lot of letters,' the postman said.
The red blood was not very nice,
The red pepper is full of spice.
Mars is the name of the planet red
Tomatoes are red that is said.
Some people have some red wine,
Especially when they sit down and dine.
So you see how important is red,
The colour of your house,
And the colour of my shed!

Sagana Sivakumaran (10)
Herington House School, Brentwood

Red Is . . .

Red is the blood
Dripping from your hand like water
From a tap.

Red is a fire
Flickering flames in the fireplace
Throwing a cosy light.

Red is Mars,
A warm glow in the night sky
Close to the moon.

Red is a tomato
Tasty, sweet, juicy and smooth.
Oh how it ripens in the sun.

Red berries and strawberries
Lovely to eat when you have a treat
It's so sweet.

Red is a sunset
That colours the clouds as it sinks
Low in the sky.

Red noses for Red Nose Day
Hang in my mind
I wish the day could come again some time.

Alice Church (9)
Herington House School, Brentwood

Rainbow

Buttercups are yellow,
Violets are blue
Tomatoes are red
And my eyes are blue!

Colours all around us
Rubies,
Sapphires
Emerald and
Diamonds
Topaz is yellow just like Saturn.

Amber is orange like the traffic lights,
Chestnut brown like coconuts.
Blazing red like the sun
When I am watching it up high.
The blue-green sea washes on your feet
The rainstorm is grey and a dirty river, black.

The colours are beautiful
For everyone to see
Everyone that is except for *me*
I'm colour-blind.

Alex Burns (9)
Herington House School, Brentwood

What Is Red?

Red is a tomato,
Juicy, smooth and sweet,
It goes well with salad,
And also with meat.

Red is a traffic light,
Which means you must stop,
Because if you don't,
You'll be caught by a cop.

Red is a raspberry,
And a strawberry too,
When you're picking your own,
Don't tread on it with your shoe.

Red is a heart,
You send to your loved one,
When you can't see them and you're apart.

Red is a pepper,
So spicy and hot,
Your mouth will burn,
If you eat the whole lot.

Red expresses feelings,
Like a hotness inside,
When you really wish you could run and hide.

Red is a show-off
No doubt about that,
It gives away
What you want to hide under the mat.

Red is fire,
Red is anger,
Be careful it might just come and get you.

Thomas Morey (9)
Herington House School, Brentwood

Red Is . . . ?

Red is a fire engine waiting to go,
Get out the way he must not go slow.
Red is a lovely and juicy cherry,
It is no wonder the birds love this berry.

Red is the colour of blood,
That runs down your face when you give it a thud.
My face is full of red flush,
When I run around in a rush.

Our postbox is red, it sits on a wall,
The letters drop in and have a long fall.
The rose is red when in full bloom
Its beautiful perfume fills the room.

Red is for danger it should make you stop,
But if you are silly it will not.
What I love best about the colour red,
It is the colour of the sheets on my lovely soft bed.

Red sky at night, shepherd's delight,
That's how the saying goes.
Red sky in the morning is the shepherd's warning,
To keep the sheep on their toes.

My mum and dad have red wine,
They sit and drink it all the time.
I have a red ruby on my ring,
It really is a pretty thing.

Red is a colour that is bright,
The first colour of the traffic light.
The robin has a bright red breast,
He is proud of his broad chest.

I like red it's plain to see,
It's definitely the colour for me.

Jessica Tuck (9)
Herington House School, Brentwood

Why We Should Love Green?

Why do people ignore green?
It's such a lovely colour.
It's very special indeed,
Just like my mother.

Green is the colour of the Earth,
Green is the colour of new birth,
Green little buds are waiting to emerge.

Green is always the sign of spring,
New herbs and unfurling leaves,
Blooming beside the clover rings.

Runner beans, vegetables flourishing all around,
While unripe green bananas are not making a sound.
Emeralds sold in business deals,
Why can't we have greens for all our meals.

Mint chocolate, ice cream melting on my tongue,
New words waiting to be sung,
If all the greens could be seen,
We would soon know why we should all love green.

Zainab Khatib (9)
Herington House School, Brentwood

Hibernating Animals

As we pass through the wood
The animals are peaceful,
They are hibernating.

I don't want to disturb them,
I will let them sleep,
The birds are in their nests,
The brown, grizzly bears
Are hibernating in the forest,
Goodnight.

Hannah Manning (9)
High March School, Beaconsfield

Flying In The Sky

I was asleep, but then I awoke,
There I was, like in my dream,
I was flying like a magic bird,
Then a bird flew past me,
I gave it some nuts
And made a friend,
Then we flew off together.

Giulia Gibbons (9)
High March School, Beaconsfield

Autumn Days

Shrivelled leaves everywhere,
The trees are as bare as a baby mouse.
A fox is stalking through the hollyhocks,
A snake is slinking through a rake.
Everywhere a carpet of crisp leaves.
Covers the gritty ground as a hedgehog scurries by.

Isabel Spoerry (8)
High March School, Beaconsfield

Winter

The snow is falling,
Dancing and prancing,
In a gentle flow.

The world is a winter wasteland,
Trees have lost their leaves,
But animals should not worry,
The world will soon be green.

Grace Brazier (9)
High March School, Beaconsfield

Autumn Wood

Some leaves are red and glow against the sky,
Upon some trees, the pines are very still,
Like small bats sleeping,
The trees are bare.

The animals are hibernating everywhere,
Hiding in crispy leaves,
Leaves are piled up all over the place,
Robins are flying overhead.

The sun is pale,
Autumn woods are full of creatures,
In the corner of my eye I see,
Two squirrels saying goodbye.

Francesca Leonard (9)
High March School, Beaconsfield

The Magic Leaf

I saw a red squirrel,
It was carrying a chestnut,
A little rabbit was hopping behind,
He was carrying a magic leaf,
It was purple and gold
And had a colourful point,
I heard the crunching of the leaves,
As a man came round the corner,
He said, 'Hello'
Then went on.

Ella Smart (9)
High March School, Beaconsfield

Autumn

The trees with their shiny leaves,
Many coloured leaves floating down,
I shuffle my way through them,
All the magnificent colours.

All these flying coloured leaves,
How I would like them to pick me up,
So I could fly away to the sky.

I love the way the leaves
Swirl round and round,
They whisper to one another,
I adore the way they whistle.

How I want to be a leaf,
I would be free,
How I would love to be free.

Sophie Palmer (9)
High March School, Beaconsfield

Autumn Leaves

In autumn the leaves fall from the trees,
They swirl and flutter down to the ground,
People walk side by side through the leaves,
I hear the leaves flying around, just like birds.

People watch, standing there,
Staring through the frosted trees,
At the leaves flying everywhere,
I see the leaves, piled up,
Right there in front of me.

Katy Hills (9)
High March School, Beaconsfield

Autumn Is My Favourite Season

It is when the bare trees sway in the strong wind,
Russet leaves fall on my head,
Berries, ripe, plump and juicy are everywhere,
I pick them up and eat them,
Foxes and squirrels hibernate, cosy and warm.

The world is full of colour!
People put on hats, scarves and gloves,
Their feet making crunching noises
In the leaves, crimson, shrivelled and crisp.

Timona Chetty (9)
High March School, Beaconsfield

Autumn Days

Autumn days when the grass is jewelled,
Squirrels sprinting on the ground,
You can feel their feet pound,
The leaves are falling, falling,
The wind is calling, calling,
Whirling, whirling,
Swirling, swirling.

Isobel McVey (9)
High March School, Beaconsfield

Autumn Days

Autumn days when the sun is shining,
Baby squirrels in the trees,
Collecting food from the yellow gold leaves,
Hedgehogs hibernating in their homes,
Conkers plopping on our heads.

Emily Stephens (8)
High March School, Beaconsfield

A Child's Autumn

The sun rolling like a huge bowling ball,
Leaves starting a hurricane,
Wind getting stronger and stronger in the boxing ring,
Rain striking my back like hedgehogs
And the cold catching me up.

Claire Read (9)
High March School, Beaconsfield

Winter's Snowman

In a blue satin hat,
Stood a snowman short and fat.

Crisp and white was the snow,
I was hoping it would never go.

When all of a sudden, the sun came out
And the snowman gave a great loud shout.

The children all came out to play,
They looked around in dismay.

Francesca White (10)
High March School, Beaconsfield

Winter

Winters are cold and white,
The ground is crisp and frozen,
The trees are bare,
No leaves at all,
They are covered from top to toe
With snow.

The ponds are frozen,
Hard as stone,
The snowdrops begin to bloom,
All drowsy looking and white.

Sophie Lomas (10)
High March School, Beaconsfield

Leaves On The Path

Leaves on the path leading to the country,
Crackle, crackle, crunch, crunch!
How I love to skip and dance,
Through the crunching, crackling leaves.

In summer, flowers bloom everywhere,
Daisies, daffodils, roses, buttercups,
Pretty as pretty, as can be.

Pom-pom hats,
Snugly gloves,
All warm and soft,
For snow so cold!

The spring brings flowers to the Earth,
The leaves are long gone,
I miss them so much!
Eight months solid until my love returns!

Georgia Hurrell (9)
High March School, Beaconsfield

I Love Autumn

Autumn glows with all the coloured leaves,
All different shapes and sizes,
Ruby, bronze, gold and orange,
Hear the sound of the breeze,
Squirrels eating nuts
And little acorns too,
Some animals are hibernating,
All these things are in autumn,
I love autumn.

Elena Monks (8)
High March School, Beaconsfield

Autumn

Inside a tiny chestnut shell,
There is a magical cell,
Full of tiny seeds,
Which fall down from the trees.

The autumn glows
And the river flows,
Gently, gently,
Red and gold reflections,
The sun in the water.

I think autumn
Is full of life,
The sun is shining, full and bright
With a slight breeze.

Annabel Johnstone (9)
High March School, Beaconsfield

Winter

Autumn was blown away by the winter wind,
Cold snow covered the road that freezing day.

Fire burning brightly, wise smiles,
Snow so deep, *huge* piles!

School telephoned me today,
They said it was a snow day.

So I watched the snowflakes dance down,
Whilst thinking about skating on the frozen pond.

Icicles, sharp as needles,
Cold as icy scales.

Slushy, pretty, swirling rain,
Dripping down the windowpane.

Jessica Kinsey (10)
High March School, Beaconsfield

Winter

I wake up and jump out of my bed,
I know a frosty morning lies ahead.

Snow on the ground like a white sheet,
Icicles pointing down at my feet.

Trees like sticks all so bare,
So cold, icy cold, but dogs don't care.

Wind is whipping around,
Buried in the snow is something to be found.

Rosanna Sasson (10)
High March School, Beaconsfield

Winter

Watch the snowflakes tipping down,
Falling on the icy town.

Snow is crunching under my feet,
It almost has a musical beat.

Drifting, dancing, sloping down,
Floating on the snow buried town.

Cottages iced with frosty lumps,
In the icing, here we jump!

Good old Santa's coming soon -
I really can't wait and it's only noon!

I'm going to skate on the frozen lake,
Just one problem - I can't brake!

I hope all this snow will stay,
I'll really cry if it goes away!

Celine Bautista (10)
High March School, Beaconsfield

Winter

The snowflakes are falling wildly,
The trees are also bare,
The ground is white,
Nobody's in sight
And my footprints are alone.

My dog is usually black,
But now she is covered
From head to tail,
In soft, white snow.

I am freezing out here in the snow,
It is minus eight degrees,
I have wrapped up cosy and warm,
In my hat, gloves and scarf.

Lucy Stephens (10)
High March School, Beaconsfield

Winter

I can hear the wind roaring,
Swirling round the snow,
Whipping at my face,
Stinging on my nose.

I can smell the dirty smoke,
Floating from the chimneys,
I can see the bare trees,
Layered in glittering white snow.

Soon it will all be over,
There'll be no snow for a year,
So I will wait patiently,
Till I can see it again.

Isabel Hutchings (10)
High March School, Beaconsfield

Winter

The snow covering the ground like a quilt
With the trees all bare,
People walking quietly, making tracks on
The floor,
Hats, gloves, coats and scarves keeping
Them warm,
Frost on all the plants so only white would
Be seen,
Snow melts, the sun has come and the
Scene has gone away.

Cristina Hall (10)
High March School, Beaconsfield

The Thunderstorm

There is a roar of thunder
As a thunderstorm begins,
Big grey clouds spread across the sky
As a thunderstorm breaks out.

The white clouds cover their ears
They don't like all the noise
That's because they're girl clouds
The big grey clouds are boys.

The girl clouds drift away
The boy clouds crash around
And spit all over the ground
Poor ground, covered in spit.

Katie Hyde-Coppock (10)
High March School, Beaconsfield

Christmas

Christmas is so wonderful,
Snow spread on the ground,
Santa is getting ready,
To give presents all around.

The Christmas tree is sparkling,
With tinsel, lighting and all,
Decorations everywhere,
Presents with all sorts of paper,
None of them are small!

Georgina Taylor (10)
High March School, Beaconsfield

A Happy Ending

Rain was pouring down the road,
Like bullets from the sky,
Pitter pattering on the roof and ground,
Lightning like a great light bulb flashing all the time.

But now the rain has come to an end,
The sun comes up once again,
All the animals of the wood are singing joyfully.

Julia Clarke (10)
High March School, Beaconsfield

Skiing

Gliding in the snow so fast,
Thinking about the pace,
Jumping, sliding, falling,
But next comes the race,
I ski, I jump,
Falling, gliding,
Oh, freezing cold hands that shiver.

Annabelle Hussey (9)
High March School, Beaconsfield

A Magical Ingredient

Look outside,
What can you see?
White glistening snow falling on me!

Snowmen all white,
With a black coal smile,
Plus an orange speckled nose
And a brown ragged hat.

Beautiful snow angels,
Dancing all around,
In white ball gowns.

These are all made,
With a special ingredient
Snow!

Joanna Jones (9)
High March School, Beaconsfield

By The Fire

I sit and watch the flames arise,
Whilst the snow falls gently,
The icicles rattle in the wind
And my snowman appears so grand!

The garden looks like Iceland
And the snow just keeps on falling
And that's when it occurs to me -
My snowman appears to be calling!

Chloe Coutts (10)
High March School, Beaconsfield

The Way Of Winter

In winter animals hibernate
And the birds stop singing,
While the trees are shaken bare by the wind
And the flowers go to sleep
Then the garden is sprinkled in snow
And not one thing is on show.

But I sit inside warm, cosy and comfortable,
Drinking hot chocolate by the fire,
While the birds scavenge for seeds and nuts
And the squirrels go to sleep
But I still like winter
Although it's cruel and harsh.

Bethaney Morrison (10)
High March School, Beaconsfield

Hedgehog In Winter

Animals are hibernating,
They're going to go to sleep,
Stuffing their little faces,
With all that they can sneak.

But one little hedgehog,
Didn't notice the frost,
The beginning of the white fields,
The trees getting lost.

The day that hedgehog noticed,
That he should be asleep,
The sun was coming up,
The snow nowhere near deep.

Isobel Kynoch (9)
High March School, Beaconsfield

Pony In The Snow

I see him,
Standing in the cold,
A warm rug on his back,
A floppy forelock covered with frost,
A pony with a certain cost,
Shiny hooves stuck firmly,
Into a blanket of white,
No one comes to see him,
Until the middle of the night
And even then, they don't bring him in,
So he is hungry and is beginning to slim,
Then a ray of light,
Kills the night
And the blanket of white is gone.

Sarah Aspland (9)
High March School, Beaconsfield

Winter Wonderland

An icy wind whirls round a tree
Stirring its bare branches,
Icicles hang from the roof,
Clear, glistening and cold,
The crisp snow crunching,
As someone walks across
Down it falls,
Like fluffs of cotton wool,
A long white carpet,
Falling from the sky,
But I sit in my sun-warm house,
With hot chocolate in my hands,
People outside are freezing cold,
But I am warm inside.

Judy Marsden (10)
High March School, Beaconsfield

Snow

All you can see is a white soft blanket,
Lying on the grass,
The children walk past,
They resist it until they burst,
They can't help it,
They must throw a snowball first.

Crunch, crunch under their feet,
As they walk across the snow,
They pick some up and throw,
It hits someone hard and drips to the floor,
The person feels it and thinks, *I'm going to throw more*,
He turns around and shouts, 'You're going to pay!'
A snowball fight's away!

Emily Burnett (9)
High March School, Beaconsfield

Falling Fast

Leaves are on the ground,
Swept up into a mould,
Crunching beneath my feet,
As I'm walking up the street,
Leaves floating down,
Like an eagle swooping low,
Leaving all the trees bare,
Wind whistling through their branches,
All the colours amaze me,
Yellow, brown, gold and red,
These are the reasons,
That I like the leaves in autumn.

Emma Curley (10)
High March School, Beaconsfield

Freezing Footsteps

When I look out of my window,
I hear freezing footsteps,
I see freezing footsteps.

When I am at school,
I see the ladies with their babies,
Making freezing footsteps.

When I am in bed,
I hear the men back from work,
Making freezing footsteps.

The next day they're all gone,
There are no more freezing footsteps.

Dara Cormican (10)
High March School, Beaconsfield

Memories

I remember when I was a little girl
My dog was outside in the wetness,
Poor little dog, I thought was he,
So I went outside and climbed a tree,
But then, after a while,
I fell you see
And got a deep cut,
My dog came up and growled,
But I went upstairs to my sister
And she said, 'You poor little thing.'

I was sad for my dog
And my sister was sad for me!

Anushka Mehta (8)
High March School, Beaconsfield

Silent Snow

When the silent snow
Whirls and twirls
And sprinkles on the ground
It is a big surprise.

I go outside to play in the snow
It is so cold
I feel like an ice cube.

Icicles glistening
And sparkling on the rooftops
Suddenly they fall
Smash! Like glass.

Then the sun comes out
Goodbye snow, hello sun.

Charlotte Hurley (11)
High March School, Beaconsfield

Winter World

In the winter when it's cold
And icicles hang strong and bold
We go outside to have some fun
For once without the sun
We build snowmen and snowballs
But then Mum calls,
'Come inside and sit by the fire,
You'll be warm so you won't tire.'
'No!' I say,
'It's much more fun to play
In the snow all day.'

Taylor Dangerfield (9)
High March School, Beaconsfield

My Playground

Before school, a couple of children are by the side of their mums,
Waiting for the bell to go,
As the teachers whistle blows, it sounds like a baby screaming,
As the bell goes, lots of children racing to their lines
Excited to start learning,
Teachers on duty, trying to tell ten boys off for swearing,
Exhausted children enjoying playing chase,
Excited children eagerly watching the race,
The silver railings stand as still as soldiers,
Trees waving in the wind,
On a wet day, the playground markings are resting,
Imagine a theme park in our playground,
As big as the Millennium stadium,
Imagine a dirt track in our playground looking like a mucky farm.

Tyler Jay Andrews (11)
Hywel Dda Junior School, Cardiff

My Playground

Rubbish rustling in the air,
Twelve Year 5s playing a game of catch,
Twenty Year 6s playing an important football match,
At 3.30 everyone runs out,
Pushing and shoving trying to get home.
As the bell goes,
Children run to their line and they chat,
Our school looks like a giant letter E,
Imagine a theme park in our playground,
As big as 50 rugby pitches,
In the future I would like to see a chocolate van,
To stop rumbling tummies,
In the future I would like to see tiring rugby training,
Every break time!
In the future I would like to see
A separate playground for boys and girls.

Cameron Smart (10)
Hywel Dda Junior School, Cardiff

Our School Poem

One wet window whistling with the wind,
Two tired children queuing for their tasty trifles,
Three thin textbooks thrown across the floor,
Four fed up teachers photocopying funny faces for art,
Five fat fish fingers frying in the pan,
Six sick children sitting by the staffroom,
Seven stupid boys flicking scrumpled paper in Class 6,
Eight annoying Alexes eating in assembly,
Nine naughty children not allowed to play netball,
Ten tired teachers trying to teach table tennis.

Class 7 & 8
Hywel Dda Junior School, Cardiff

My Playground

Children running around the playground,
Like little rats running around the sewers,
The silver railings stand as still as statues,
Ten cheeky choppy Chelseas chewing chunky cherries,
Chattering cheeky children sit on the wall,
With wet, woolly warm white coats,
Before school, delivery men bring food to the
Kitchen for the cooks,
On a wet day, rain falling down like leaves
Coming off the tree,
At 3.30 children barge past like bumper cars
Bumping into each other,
Excited children have a fun race,
All the others playing a game called chase,
Imagine a dirt bike track,
As long and as high as the Great Wall of China,
Imagine a water slide,
As twirly as a twister,
Imagine a trampoline,
As bouncy as a bouncy ball.

Chelsea Fenn (10)
Hywel Dda Junior School, Cardiff

Colour Poem

Red is a sweet strawberry,
Blue is the calm sea,
White is a piece of paper,
Green is a bit of a leaf,
Brown is a lump of chocolate,
Orange is a cheeping bird,
Gold is a gift for Jesus,
Violet is a long bit of tinsel,
Cream is a big settee,
Burgundy is a start car,
Bronze is a shiny metal,
Sapphire is a calm sky,
Indigo is a huge bruise,
Diamond is a sparkling ring,
Emerald is waving grass in the sun.

Ben Moore (9)
Hywel Dda Junior School, Cardiff

Colour Poem

Red is a delicate rose,
Blue is a clean ocean,
White is a calm cloud,
Green is a straight field,
Brown is a flat piece of mud,
Orange is a chunk of orange,
Silver is sparkling load of money,
Gold is a diamond ring,
Violet is a fine tinsel,
Cream is a thick milkshake,
Burgundy is a helpful hairdresser,
Bronze is a clean medal,
Sapphire is a soft sky,
Indigo is dark of a night,
Diamond is a sparkling ring,
Emerald is waving grass in the sun.

Dyllon Thomas (9)
Hywel Dda Junior School, Cardiff

My Playground

Children having fun like little babies,
A group of boys playing rugby thinking they are Jonny Wilkinson,
Mr Rees shouting enough to be a lion,
Gabrielle kissing as sloppy as a dog's tongue,
All the teachers at school shouting breaking all the windows,
Sophie whistling like train's wheels coming by,
Jack swearing like a man on a building site,
A group of girls playing kiss chase in the classroom,
Two girls dancing thinking they're on Top of the Pops,
Shane screaming enough to be an eel,
Moody boys playing kiss chase getting all confused,
A group of kids skipping catching the rope and tripping,
I would like a hairdresser to have different styles every day,
I wish we can have a pool so we could have *fun*!
I wish we had a smoochy room, so we could have a little kiss,
And our boyfriends wouldn't be shy because they
Could just come up to us and give us a kiss like we do, *not*!

Gemma Wozencroft (10)
Hywel Dda Junior School, Cardiff

Colour Poem

Red is a sweet strawberry,
Blue is shiny water,
White is hot rays of the sun,
Green is a tree that is dark,
Brown is a hard fool,
Orange is a sun that is setting,
Silver is a moon that is shining,
Gold is a medal for the brave,
Violet is a purple flower,
Cream is a bowl of ice cream,
Burgundy is a 3rd winning medal,
Bronze is the dark, dark soil,
Sapphire is the ocean that is wide.

Dominy Hale (9)
Hywel Dda Junior School, Cardiff

My Playground

Boys fighting like two boxers scrapping over girls,
Boys playing football zooming for the ball like a racing car,
Children being silent playing hide-and-seek,
Kids screaming like the wind at a footie match,
Crisp bags popping up and down in the air like a jumping kangaroo,
With their contents crunching like people stepping on autumn leaves,
Girls and boys playing Twister getting tangled up,
Little youngsters playing hopscotch jumping here and there,
Planes like enormous flying birds in the sky leaving
                                       prints as they fly by,
The field attracts bugs to it like a scent of a flower attracts bees,
The sun like a big orange light bulb brightening people's days,
Very hot teachers playing tennis slashing balls everywhere,
I'd like cinemas and shops so I could watch the latest,
I'd love a swimming pool so I could practise my swimming,
I wish there were food machines so I would have a
                                       choice of what to eat,
I wish there were roller coasters so I could have fun.

Sheekilah Jones (10)
Hywel Dda Junior School, Cardiff

As Strong As . . .

As strong as a giant lifting up ten houses,
As weak as a kitten when it's first born,
As loud as two babies screaming in the house,
As quiet as the leaves falling off the trees,
As bright as the golden sun in the sky,
As dull as the sky when it rains,
As rough as the strong ground when you fall,
As smooth as a petal from a flower,
As fierce as a nasty dog biting you,
As gentle as you when you breathe.

Jessica Jones (8)
Hywel Dda Junior School, Cardiff

My Playground

Teachers standing like statues in a palace,
Antony's footsteps sounding like thunder,
Children swearing like Ozzy Osbourne,
People playing rugby like rhinos,
Children screaming like ghosts,
Joshua's crisps crunching like earthquakes,
Children hanging around like monkeys in a tree,
Kids gorging on cakes like snakes,
Teams charging trying to dodge the bulldog,
Tree shaped monsters out to scare us,
Kids having dodge the ball jumping to miss the ball,
Friends playing football fighting for the ball,
Children playing kiss chase pulling a face,
Footballs bouncing like bombs,
I wish there were no girls to give sloppy kisses,
And a massive spider web to hang from.

James Coles-Bessant (10)
Hywel Dda Junior School, Cardiff

As Strong As . . .

As strong as a scent of a rose,
As weak as a worm trying to get away from a bird.

As loud as a baby crying,
As quiet as a fox stalking its prey.

As bright as the sun on a hot sunny day,
As dull as a cold rainy day.

As rough as the carpet when you have no shoes on,
As smooth as a newborn kitten.

As fierce as a lion roaring in the jungle,
As gentle as a petal from a flower.

Jordanne Wilson (9)
Hywel Dda Junior School, Cardiff

My Playground

Shouting loudly girls skipping like bouncy kangaroos,
Mad big boys playing rugby thinking they're really cool,
Crisp packets spread like birds' wings on the floor,
Mothers walking children to school like a daisy chain,
Rubbish bins standing like guards around a special place,
Naughty children swearing like dockers because they're in a mood,
Children whistling like a train going under a tunnel
           because they want people's attention,
Children screaming like hungry seagulls because they
                              want some food,
Children crying producing little streams because they
                              got hit by the ball,
Little kiddies giving sloppy kisses because they've been dared,
Year 6s playing Pop Idol cracking the school windows,
Smelly little children hanging around the toilets like
           statues because they are cold,
I wish boys would give the girls a ramp show and
           show their latest moves.
A fashion shop for the girls and a stage to do a little performance,
We'd have a gum machine and I'd chew it all day long,
I wish we had a roller coaster that was higher than the Eiffel Tower.

Charlotte Devine (11)
Hywel Dda Junior School, Cardiff

As Strong As . . .

As strong as a scent from a garden rose,
As weak as a newborn kitten sleeping in a bed,
As loud as music blasting in my bedroom,
As quiet as a shark swimming up to its prey,
As bright as a sun in a boiling hot desert,
As dull as the night itself,
As rough as a fossil that's been in the ground,
As smooth as a petal of a flower in the garden,
As fierce as lions in a middle of a fight,
As gentle as a baby's bum.

Lucy Macnamara (8)
Hywel Dda Junior School, Cardiff

My Playground

Two tall teachers playing tennis toppling over toes,
Planes like clouds always travelling somewhere,
Jessica kissing Alex like anteaters,
Screaming children skipping, scrapping their shoes,
Teachers like birds waiting to catch their prey,
Chelsea arguing over who looks the best like stars on the telly,
Children shouting like they're afraid of seagulls,
Bells ringing like money dropping on metal,
Parents swearing like Ozzy Osbourne in a bad mood,
Gates like doors waiting to be opened,
Children arguing over who will be friends with
                        who like me and my sister,
Footballs like birds moving in the sky,
Children hiding in mob with dirty gobs,
Mums knitting after school like children's nans.

Katie Pounds (11)
Hywel Dda Junior School, Cardiff

Colour Poem

Red is a sugary strawberry,
Blue is the bright sky,
White is the patchy clouds,
Green is the smelly trees,
Brown is the dark woods,
Orange is a squeezy orange,
Silver is a jar full of money,
Gold is piece of a little penny,
Violet is a really posh car,
Cream is a bowl of ice cream,
Burgundy is a red wine,
Bronze is a penny clean,
Sapphire is a dark colour,
Indigo is a dark night.

Lauren Price (10)
Hywel Dda Junior School, Cardiff

My Playground

Girls are shouting, 'Mob, mob 1, 2, 3, you're out!' like a lion's roar.
Clouds drift by in the sky like big fluffy teddy bears.
Grass swaying in the wind like a child waving
                      goodbye to their mothers.
Crisp bags drift around like beef and onion flavoured birds.
Balls kicked by boys bouncing around like crazy kangaroos.
While some children are cackling like strangled cats by the toilets.
Teachers timing our fun while enjoying their warm cups of tea.
I like laying on the grass like an independent lion,
Sometimes I sprint around like Kelly Holmes,
I like to act like a little puppy when I'm
Messing with my friends and then laze around like a sleepy, lazy dog,
I wish there were only sensible people so *no* fights,
And Year 6 only in the playground with no little people annoying us,
I'd love *no rules* so we can go mental!
And an enormous theme park and cinema screens
And sounds so we can enjoy play even more!

Emma Laver (10)
Hywel Dda Junior School, Cardiff

As Strong As . . .

As strong as 1,000 horses pulling a cart,
As weak as a newborn kitten in its bed.

As loud as a car with loud music,
As quiet as a tortoise walking to its food.

As bright as a hot and bright sunshine,
As dull as a wrestler losing a fight.

As rough as a big rough man in a fight,
As smooth as a cat when you smooth it.

As fierce as a tiger groaning at you for food,
As gentle as a kitten purring at you.

Jessica Thomas (9)
Hywel Dda Junior School, Cardiff

My Playground

Friends hate playing Red Rover cause they struggle to get through,
Boys shouting, playing kiss chase but they have no other choice,
Lots of children moving, a herd of sheep following on the top field,
Your shadow is like your clone waiting to take your place,
Gates like jail cells keeping you the prisoner in jail,
People playing hide-and-seek while resting now and then,
Boys happily playing football tackling everyone,
While friends fight over partners like elephants
                              stamping on the ground,
People kissing as sloppy as your dog when he licks you,
Footsteps creeping like people when they try not to be found,
Children cough like cats do when they have a fur ball in winter,
As spongeballs fly like spaceships falling from the sky,
I wish the boys were on top field so they would not annoy the girls,
With their footballs flying everywhere, I wish we could have
A climbing frame with *no* boys allowed,
But at last I just want everyone to get along.

Gabrielle Evans (10)
Hywel Dda Junior School, Cardiff

As Strong As . . .

As strong as a snake taking down its prey in its jaws,
As weak as a man picking up a tonne,
As loud as an elephant trumpeting its trunk,
As quiet as a chick sneaking to its nest,
As bright as a torch shining in the night,
As dull as the sun fading into the night,
As rough as some sandpaper scraping the wall,
As smooth as some paper getting written on,
As fierce as a tiger looking for its prey,
As gentle as a puppy playing with a baby.

Joseph Connolly (9)
Hywel Dda Junior School, Cardiff

My Playground

Before school Mr Stowell and Hywel clean up,
Making our playground safe,
On a wet day the puddly playground looks so
Different through the wet windows,
As the bell goes mad, children rush out for fresh air,
Scarves swishing and swinging in the wind,
As children play chase,
Chattering children playing truth or dare,
Teachers shouting 'Crazy Bear!'
Coats lying in piles,
Looking like black bags waiting to be collected,
Children back in class allowing birds to tidy up all the
                                        leftover crisps,
Seagulls swooping down eating salty and spicy
                                        crisps in the playground,
Houses hovering high up on the hill can be seen,
Imagine a swimming pool in the middle of our playground,
Like the enormous deep blue sea,
Imagine a breakfast shop in our playground,
As busy as McDonald's.

Jade Edmunds (11)
Hywel Dda Junior School, Cardiff

As Strong As . . .

As strong as a muscleman picking up a rock,
As weak as wind blowing in your hair,
As loud as a rooster crowing in the morning,
As quiet as a bird looking for worms,
As bright as the sun in the morning light,
As dull as the sky when the rain has been falling,
As rough as fossils dug in the ground,
As smooth as a pebble on the beach,
As fierce as a fox looking for his prey,
As gentle as a baby's bottom.

Charlotte Friis (9)
Hywel Dda Junior School, Cardiff

My Playground

Boys playing football, no one's scoring any goals.
Kids playing Twister tied up in a knot.
Girls having a game of hopscotch, hopping like kangaroos.
Air like water floating in the sky on a breezy day.
Boys playing rugby, well I'm scoring all the tries like Jonny Wilkinson.
Grass like green spikes, if you touch them you'll get hurt.
Fighting like stones banging against each other
                              but making nothing better.
Footballs like boulders coming at you off a mountain.
Children speeding like leopards having a race in the jungle.
Singing by Shane like a screech running through my ears.
Kids playing bulldogs, like crazy elephants in a stampede.
Girls arguing like mad cats.
I wish we had a cinema so we could see the new movies out
And a sweet machine so I could eat sweets every day.

Anthony Somersall (11)
Hywel Dda Junior School, Cardiff

Colour Poem

Red is a juicy strawberry,
Blue is a cold sea,
White is a sheet of paper,
Green is as soft as paper,
Brown is a bucket of mud,
Orange is a bright jumper,
Silver is a shiny coin,
Gold is a medal for life,
Violet is a fish in the sea,
Cream is a relaxed home,
Burgundy is a car of hope,
Bronze is a purse full of money,
Sapphire is a deep sea,
Indigo is a dark night,
Diamond is a precious love,
Emerald is a green car.

Bethan Sterio (9)
Hywel Dda Junior School, Cardiff

My Playground!

Silly Sophie skipping on the ground,
Girls kissing boys like huge sloppy dogs,
Gates swinging open as the wind flows by,
Terrific teachers teaching tennis,
Children cracking jokes like the birds in the morning,
Houses as towering as giraffes' necks,
Sun drifting over you like a ball of fire,
Terrible teachers slamming the ball in tennis,
Clouds rolling around like Little Bo Peep's sheep,
Police sirens out in the street.
I wish there were no boys because they don't play fair
And a pool so we could practise swimming.
I wish there was a theme park so we could go on the roller coaster
　　　　　　　　　　　　　　　　　　　　　when we want to.
I'd like Man Utd players so they could coach us every day
And a gum machine so we could blow bubbles as big as an
　　　　　　　　　　　　　　　　　　elephant's backside.

Paige Chick (11)
Hywel Dda Junior School, Cardiff

As Strong As . . .

As strong as the Olympic rowers reaching the finishing line,
As weak as a kitten that's just been born.

As loud as the supporters at a football match,
As quiet as a mouse going for the cheese.

As bright as the sun in the hottest desert,
As dull as a rainy day in winter.

As rough as an elephant's skin,
As smooth as a baby rabbit's white smooth fur.

As fierce as a lion tearing up his prey,
As gentle as a wisp of wind on my face.

Laura Griffiths (9)
Hywel Dda Junior School, Cardiff

My Playground

Teachers in the hall humming like howling dogs.
Broccoli trees crunchy and green dreaming in the breeze.
Clouds like marshmallows in a clear blue sky.
All the boys playing Red Rover, one just fell all the way over.
Funny, fit boys frantically playing football.
The sun like the yolk in my egg.
Kids kissing like messy dogs.
Kind, cool girls kindly playing polo.
Children like ants when scurrying on the floor.
Big, bad bullies barging in bulldogs.
Balls like a full moon in the middle of the night.
Children laughing at hilarious hyenas.
I wish there were no boys because boys begin fights
And more time to play outside instead of doing work.
I wish we had roller coasters in our playground so we can
                                        have more fun
And a cinema screen so we can just watch TV.

Chelsea Bedford (11)
Hywel Dda Junior School, Cardiff

Puzzle Poem

I have two arms but no legs,
I move quite often,
I am in most classrooms or houses,
I come in all different shapes and sizes.

What am I?

A: a clock.

Amy Jones (11)
Hywel Dda Junior School, Cardiff

My Playground

Teachers like super spies watching your every move.
Kids fighting like vultures for the last scraps of food.
Teachers shouting at naughty children like a volcano about to erupt.
Girls skipping like bouncy frogs jumping down and up.
Boys hanging around like bats in the daytime.
Children weeping enough to create a monsoon.
Apples crunching like an earthquake as they're being bitten and . . .
Balls bouncing like bombs heading for you.
Kids screaming like a train coming into the station.
Friends playing bulldogs racing for the safety point.
Girls performing handstands trying not to fall over.
Children moaning like the Mona Lisa hung up on the wall.
I wish there was a roller coaster to have a ride on and . . .
A cinema to watch the latest screenings.
I wish there were bike ramps to have a little go on.

Joshua Parsons (11)
Hywel Dda Junior School, Cardiff

As Strong As . . .

As strong as elephants pulling an aeroplane to the station.
As weak as wind blowing your hair.
As loud as fireworks going off in the air.
As quiet as a mouse creeping for some cheese.
As bright as the sun in the morning light.
As dull as rain blowing in the sea.
As rough as fossils just dug up from the ground.
As smooth as writing on a piece of paper.
As fierce as a grizzly bear in the forest.
As gentle as a baby's bottom.

Kim Powell
Hywel Dda Junior School, Cardiff

My Playground

Up in the sky is a helicopter over Hywel Dda Junior School.
Teachers trying to tell children to stop running in the corridor.
Lots of excited children trying to win the race.
Careless children trying to do up their laces.
Before school Mr Stowel makes sure all is safe for us
                                    especially no glass.
At 3.30 as the school doors open
Children rush out to show they're proud
To present certificates to their mums and dads.
Imagine a trampoline in the playground as bouncy as a sofa.
Locks on gates to protect our property from people coming in.
Imagine an ice rink in our playground, as white as a cloud
What a fun playground this would be.
Out in the playground ten terrible children line up
                            when the fire bell goes.

Leanne Stimpson (11)
Hywel Dda Junior School, Cardiff

Our Playground

A delicious smell from the kitchen makes us drool.
The boys skilfully kicking the ball to make them look cool.
Imagine an ice rink in our playground.
As glittery as the crystal on Mount Everest.
Before school excited children meet, ready to learn.
Children chatting and chasing their mates.
Friends fighting furiously for the football.
Children back in class looking through the window.
Crisp packets flying around like swirling leaves.
Scrumptious smell slipping silently under the squeaky kitchen door,
Floating silently.
On a wet day children looking out on the playground,
Waiting for the sun to come out
At home time mums and dads wait like standing penguins.
At 3.30 children race through doors like racing dogs running home.

Leanne Browning (11)
Hywel Dda Junior School, Cardiff

My Playground

Scrumptious smells slipping silently under the squeaky kitchen door,
Floating to the children.
Girls talking to teachers and teasing their friends.
Two teachers chatting, standing by the wall.
Delicious smells of sausages wafting through the hall.
As the bell goes the door opens and children run out ready to play.
On a wet day, the playground is slippery and shining.
Big bins bursting full of bottles and bags of crisps
                                      blowing over the playground.
Girls skipping slowly, singing songs.
Nine naughty netballers aiming for the net.
Before school excited children lined up ready to work.
At 3.30 everyone runs out of school to see their mums and dads.
Imagine a swimming pool in our playground as long as a limo.
In the future I imagine a chocolate shop for us.
I imagine a set of swings to play on.
I imagine an ice cream machine for us all to use.
In the future I would like everyone to play nicely together.

Emma Russell (10)
Hywel Dda Junior School, Cardiff

Our Playground

Before school children lining up to go and do some work.
As the bell goes people rushing out of the classroom
                                      wanting to buy tuck.
Happy children hopping on the squares of the playground.
Children back in class watching seagulls swooping
                                      after the leftover crisps and cakes.
Big bins bursting full of bottles and empty bags of crisps
                                      blowing over the playground.
At 3.30 children racing to show their mums and dads their artwork.
Imagine bouncing like a kangaroo hopping through a field.
Imagine an ice rink in our playground as cold as the North Pole.
Imagine a swimming pool in our playground, as deep as the sea.
Imagine a dirt bike track, too long to measure.

Jason O'Brien (10)
Hywel Dda Junior School, Cardiff

My Playground

Boys doing keepy uppys thinking they're Rooney
Crisps crunch like waves crashing together on a stormy night.
The school shaped like a capital E when you look down from the sky.
People swearing like Ozzy Osbourne when his wife
                              was having an affair.
Year 6 mucky fighting, thinking they're hard.
Kids hugging each other when they need a pal.
Floor markings like games on a playing board.
Air as clear as crystals in a jewellery box sitting on my desk.
Children bawling as loud as elephants marching through the jungle.
Children answering back like smelly li'l dockers
                              because they think they're cool.
Lads making a den out of grass when they need somewhere to hide.
Birdies yelping like my bro when he stumped his big toe.
Teachers smoking in the staffroom when the kids are out to play.
I wish we had longer play so I could play with my mates.
I wish we could have all our working time just playing football.

Gabrielle Newing (11)
Hywel Dda Junior School, Cardiff

As Strong As . . .

As strong as 1,000 horses pulling a coach.
As weak as a man picking up a chair.
As loud as a stereo blasting full volume.
As quiet as a baby sleeping.
As bright as the sun shining across the sea.
As dull as a torch.
As rough as someone's hair once they haven't brushed it.
As smooth as your clothes once they have been ironed.
As fierce as a tiger growling.
As gentle as a kitten purring.

Ffiôn Bisatt (9)
Hywel Dda Junior School, Cardiff

My Playground

In the playground I like annoying my cousins
Because they're fun to play with.
I like playing football with the boys
Because they give me good tackles for when I play a girls'
                                          football match.
Playing my recorder for St David's Day when I play to the school.
Worn out girls enjoying skipping,
They are happy because they're winning.
Friends happily playing Red Rover, someone picked a lucky clover.
Most of my friends are happily playing mob,
When they're on they like to sob.
Flowers like heads bobbing back and forth in the wind.
Railings like bars in a prison cell with a metal door.
Clouds like marshmallow shapes in the sky.
Children swearing like Ozzy Osbourne on a good day.
Crunching like a bar of Crunchie crunching in someone's mouth.
Screaming in a opera with a fat lady singing.
No boys to give sloppy kisses.
Have a cinema to watch new films every minute of every day.
Phone shops to buy a better phone every day.

Christina Mitchell (11)
Hywel Dda Junior School, Cardiff

My Playground

Two friends playing Twister, they hope the fun never ends,
While six girls skip energetically, counting how many loops they do.
Groups of friends playing netball, trying their best to help their team.
Other children love playing mob and having stacks of fun.
Grass like green, sharp needles pointing up towards the sky,
While teachers stand like guards,
Watching the children, keeping them safe.
Houses like enormous heads keeping you warm inside,
As clouds float by like big fluffy sheep,
Waiting for the wind to blow them away.
Children are hanging around like bats ready for their midday snooze.
Meanwhile friends tell jokes as if they are on a talent show.
Enemies are disagreeing about who is the handsome one,
As angry as can be.
As kids kiss, as disgusting as an old mouldy burger.
I wish there were no boys to get on girls' nerves
And a swimming pool to try out the new skills I've learnt.
I'd like a sweet machine so I could have treats to eat
                                              which are delicious!
No rain, just warmth would be fun,
So we could go out every play and lunchtime.

Hayley Prowse (11)
Hywel Dda Junior School, Cardiff

My Playground

Crisp bags like ghosts flying around you in the playground.
Apples crunching, crisps being stamped on in the yard.
Children and teachers arguing like cats and dogs.
Trees like hands gripping your back to scare you after school,
Thinking people will kill you.
Planes like bombs attacking us in war make me feel sad and scared.
Children pretending to be the army
Like the general that says it's barmy.
Air sends shivers down your back and spine in the playground.
Doors creaking like fingers clicking.
Year 3 approaching like Kelly Holmes in the playground.
Children wailing like a vampire sucking your blood.
Police sirens in the street as loud as James crunching sweets.
I wish there were shady kissing rooms for people to snog each other.
Cinema screen to look at the latest movies.
Mobile shop so people can have phones.
Just Year 6 and 5 in the playground
Because Year 3 and 4 try to punch Year 6 and 5.

Shane Pritchard (11)
Hywel Dda Junior School, Cardiff

My Playground

Ten boys playing football hoping to score a goal.
Six silly girls telling jokes and giggling like hyenas.
Children moaning like babies because they got put in detention.
Girls getting dirty on the top field like pigs in a pigsty.
Teachers chatting like chatterboxes about what they watch at home.
Mr Rees shouting like an elephant in the yard.
Wind puffing like people breathing hard after exercise.
I like playing football because it keeps me fit.
I like talking because I like telling people my secrets.
I like skipping because I can jump up and down
                               and beat my score every time.
I like catch because it makes me laugh when people grab me
And sprinting like Kelly Holmes because it's good fun.
I wish there were no boys to get on my nerves
And no railings around the school, so we could be free.
I'd like a pool to chill when we get hot and bothered.
And I'd like it to be open all day and night,
Just Year 6 girls and our family are allowed in it.

Stephanie Truman (11)
Hywel Dda Junior School, Cardiff

My Playground

Crisps crunch making a noise like dragons biting on
                                                anything they see,
Skipping ropes like slithering snakes as children skip with them,
Skipping ropes smacking on the ground as they rotate
                                                round and round,
Six Year 6 girls happily hopping along the hopscotch,
Loud boys telling jokes making people giggle,
A group of boys playing mob having a wicked time,
Girls enjoying kiss chase and boys having a running race,
Happy girls kissing boys, giving them all their love,
Giant round footballs flying through the air,
Like juicy, juicy plums,
Girls arguing over silly things,
Naughty children swearing like dockers thinking they're all hard,
Teachers chatting to each other having a long conversation
                                              about naughty children,
I wish there was a theme park so I could have more fun with
My friends at playtime.
And I want a sweet shop full of free chocolate and
Candy so I can eat them all day long,
Build ramps so I could bring my bike to school
And enjoy every minute of my playtime,
With a cool clothes shop so me and all of my mates
Could have a fashion show.

Sophie Newsham (11)
Hywel Dda Junior School, Cardiff

My Playground

Teachers are like your guardians, staring at every move you make.
Little lunatics dashing through the air
As if they are in a crazy running race.
Balls like stones getting booted through the air.
A group of four girls devising a dance.
People fighting like sumo wrestlers with people cheering them on.
Year 6s bashing the little Year 3s like karate kids.
Boys telling jokes like they are desperate to get a valentine.
Clouds of white candyfloss flying in the air.
Flowers like pop star dancers swaying in the sky.
Five football players finding they can't play
Because they are wrapped in layers of fur.
Ten terrible tennis players thinking they are Tim Henman.
I wish there was a fairground so I wouldn't get bored at playtime.
I would love a sports centre so I could practice my
                                    football technique and become a star.
Play with Man Utd players so I could catch up with the latest goss
                                        with my cousin Giggs
And a resting room would be the best that way I could rest in peace.

Ciera Honey (11)
Hywel Dda Junior School, Cardiff

The Simpsons

Homer is fat and Lisa is clever,
Marge is a cooking expert,
I could watch this show forever and ever,
Homer would kill for a slice of tart!

Then there is Maggie, the speechless baby,
Who never utters a word,
I don't think she'll speak, but then again maybe,
For Bart to get an A would be absurd!

This show is the best, it's on at 7 o'clock,
Though on 4 it's on at six,
Nelson the bully, everyone he does mock,
It sometimes comes on, on Sky Mix!

Sometimes it's mysterious, sometimes it's strange,
Though the missions are always unfurled,
When I'm watching TV the channel won't change,
Cos it's the best bloomin' show in the *world!*

Euan McIntyre (11)
Iona Primary School, Argyll

Winter

The snow is like paper,
Shredded,
Then thrust upon the world.

The children are like mice,
Scurrying,
Looking for somewhere to hide.

The day is like ice,
Freezing,
But tremendously fun.

The bed covers are like long jumpers,
Warm,
And very, very cosy and soft.

Laura Channing (11)
Ledbury Primary School, Ledbury

My Plan To Save The Planet

Save the planet!

I'm an unhappy dustbin
As black as the night
All I do is sit here
And collect dust
I should sit here
And collect rubbish

I want to be . . .
Smelly and horrible,
A dustbin should be
As smelly as a drain
Dustbins are like black holes
Sucking up everything in their paths

Fill me up
Until I spill.
Don't dig up the earth
And landfill.
Let the worms get to work
And eat the things that make us ill.

Daisy Yeates (10)
Longdon St Mary's CE (VA) Primary School, Tewkesbury

I Am A Light Bulb

I am a light bulb, I am a light bulb.
I get wasted, people never turn me off.
All they need to do is hit the switch.
There are hundreds of people that waste electricity.
They just don't turn us off.
We get wasted straight away
Then another light bulb comes and takes my place,
Has my fun and then disappears.

Save the world, hit the switch.

Rosie Woodward (10)
Longdon St Mary's CE (VA) Primary School, Tewkesbury

What Am I?

I'm fed every day to stock up my tummy,
To feed the plants when it's sunny.
What am I?

*Crash, bash, clash, bang,
As I'm emptied for the year*
What am I?

Smelly smells come
From my tummy.
What am I?

I help the environment and I help the plants
Grow strong and healthy.
What am I?

I'm as hungry as a horse
And I eat all sorts of food.
What am I?

A: I'm a compost bin.

Charlotte Webber (11)
Longdon St Mary's CE (VA) Primary School, Tewkesbury

Robin

Robin with a chest
As red as a cherry
Pecking for a juicy wiggly worm.

Robin flies
With fluffy feathers
Laying an egg in a nice new nest.

Small robin
Sing a song,
'Cheep cheep,' baby robin calls.

Guy Vickery (10)
Longdon St Mary's CE (VA) Primary School, Tewkesbury

I'm A Banana

I'm a banana from the Bahamas
With the moon shining bright at night
I'm a bit like a flower, bursting with power.

I've been picked and peeled and eaten
I've been flung down on the floor
I'm all brown and bruised
Just like a bear.

I'm as sloppy as a slug
Slidey and smelly
I'm the colour of apple juice
All sticky and slippy.

I've been put in a wormery for over a year
With thousands of teeny weeny worms
Who've nibbled me to compost
And now I'm on a carrot patch and crushed!

Isabella Thompson (10)
Longdon St Mary's CE (VA) Primary School, Tewkesbury

The Park

The park is trashed,
Full of litter all smashed,
Sharp fences are like knives,
Don't spare any lives
The park is for fun,
That's not what you've done!

The bins aren't used
To keep rubbish in,
They are empty and hungry
They are dark and dim.
This park is a place,
Made of misery and sorrow,
Let's hope you change it by tomorrow!

Sophia Franklin (10)
Longdon St Mary's CE (VA) Primary School, Tewkesbury

A Day In The Life Of A Hungry Black Bin

I'm as black as the night,
But as light as a feather,
There's hardly anything for the bin men,
Sometimes there's nothing at all,
My owners never feed me,
Oh, I'm so hungry!

Look at all those recycling bins,
They're getting fed much more than me,
I'm only fed plastic and packaging,
I never get recyclable things,
I'm all alone in the world these days,
Oh, I'm so hungry!

There should only be one type of bin,
The good old, loyal black bin,
Those eco bins are as green as grass,
(Which I think is an absolutely disgusting colour),
But I'm as black as the night,
Oh, I'm so hungry!

I'm a hungry animal,
Eating anything I can get,
Old plastic tastes like hard, stale bread,
I'm a hungry stomach,
Eating all the waste,
Oh, I'm so hungry!

I used to get paper,
I used to get glass,
I wish old recycling was all in the past,
I'm a bottomless hole,
You can never fill me up,
Oh, I'm so hungry!

I'm an eating machine,
I might gobble you up,
I'm a black plastic monster,
It's really not fair,
I'll get sick and die if they don't feed me soon,
Oh, I'm so hungry!

Laura Scott (11)
Longdon St Mary's CE (VA) Primary School, Tewkesbury

Birds

A bird flies like a plane.
As careful as a pilot.
Eats nuts like crazy,
Ruffled feathers blowing in the wind.
Birds sing beautiful sweet-sounding songs.

Hedges are like homes
So don't cut trees or hedges.
If you have to, avoid nesting season
And put bird feeders out.

Put more bird boxes out,
Give homes to birds
And don't spray fields.

If you do all of this
Lots of birds will live.
So do at least two or three of these things
To stop birds dying.

Jaimie Sinclair (10)
Longdon St Mary's CE (VA) Primary School, Tewkesbury

The Careless Driver

I am the driver of the sleek orange Ferrari.
I am speeding down the country roads in my 600mph Ferrari.
I am using too much fuel in my spluttering, choking car.
I am throwing out pollution and I don't care.

I am clogging up the roads and I don't care.
I am using thick, black, smelly oil in my thick, black, smelly engine.
There's too much traffic in town,
'Get out of the way, this car can kill.'
My thick fumes fill up the sky destroying the ozone layer
And I still don't care.
My big, fat tyres are burning up the road
When they run out, I don't care.
I just fling them on the tyre mountain.
I am the driver of the sleek orange Ferrari.
I am speeding down the country roads and I just don't care.

Christian Cox (10)
Longdon St Mary's CE (VA) Primary School, Tewkesbury

The Light Bulb People

We've got a hat that plugs us in
And we start off very, very dim
When we are turned on.

We're like sparkling diamonds
And as shiny as the sun
As yellow as a daffodil
We're so very bright.

We come in different shapes and sizes
Square, rectangles
Short, long and round
With a swirly filament inside.

All my friends are eco-friendly
Because we like the world
We are the light bulb people
We light up your whole world.

Jack Larner (10)
Longdon St Mary's CE (VA) Primary School, Tewkesbury

Recycle Bin

I'm so hungry, so hungry indeed,
I will always get peckish,
So come on and feed me,
Chomp! Chomp! Chomp!

Give me bananas or pyjamas
Crash!
Give me a boot or some fruit
And let me eat your rubbish.

Pears are so sweet
And I care for some wheat
Peelings are as wet as a puddle
Yum!

I'm as fat as a hippo
Full of waste
And I love the taste.

Carianne Martin (11)
Longdon St Mary's CE (VA) Primary School, Tewkesbury

The Crisp Bag Poem

Crunchy, crackly and smells like vinegar,
Littering is illegal,
People drop litter.

Floating away to different places,
Flying away with the outdoor wind,
Soaking wet in the rain and only sometimes in the bin.

All wet and soaking with mud,
Useless, screwed pieces of litter,
Caught up in some hedges.

A little child picks it up and runs home,
The litter is so smelly, he drops it,
A boring, smelly crisp packet,
No use to anyone.

Harvey Carter (9)
Longdon St Mary's CE (VA) Primary School, Tewkesbury

The Calling Of The Polar Bear

His breath is like a warm summer breeze
His claws are sharper than a lion's
He hunts and grunts
His tongue is longer than a giraffe's.

His fur is softer than the softest feather,
Cute, cuddly, ripping claws
He snuffles and sniffs but he scares and strikes
This bear needs help like a patient in a hospital.

He has the swimming skills of a penguin
His teeth are as sharp as daggers
So you'd better pause before you cause
The home of a bear to turn to thin air.

His home is icier than a crisp winter's day
Yet it's melting faster than ice being thrown into a fire
By the power of oil you force nature to toil
Until it weeps without a wink of sleep.

Victoria Houghton (10)
Longdon St Mary's CE (VA) Primary School, Tewkesbury

Frog

A fast, fat frog
As bouncy as a cricket
As croaky as a cuckoo clock
A slippery, slimy frog
With a tongue as long as a stick
As wet as a fish on the deck
As green as a blade of grass.

Samuel Carter (9)
Longdon St Mary's CE (VA) Primary School, Tewkesbury

The Rubbish Bin

Please, somebody feed me
I'm underfed, I'm starving.
I'm as hungry as a hyena.

I'm bored all day,
Dull and flat.
I feel invisible and hidden,
Empty like the black hole
And redundant.
No job.

My recycling friend is full but I'm not
And my tummy is rumbling all day.
I'm really excited,
Is it dinner time yet?
I'm a greedy bin.

I'm so sad
As sad as a broken heart.
I feel as light as a downy feather
But I'm still as dry as a desert.

I'm so hungry,
So sad
Because the public are recycling,
Re-using and reducing
And a boring life my future life will be.

Holly Barrett (10)
Longdon St Mary's CE (VA) Primary School, Tewkesbury

Turn Me Off!

I start off black
Like a big, fat bat
Then going on bright
Like a star in the night
When I am bright
I'm not like the night
But when I am black
It feels like a fight.

I'm lighting up the room
For a girl over there
My glow creates a shimmer
Of gold in her hair.
When she is watching TV
I help her see.

My heart is now scorching
Like a candle flame
Just a simple flick of my switch
Will make me happy.
It's been many hours now
Since I leapt into action
So please, please turn me off
So I can have a happy day
Because I will have lots of energy saved.

Alice Kerrigan (10)
Longdon St Mary's CE (VA) Primary School, Tewkesbury

Muddled Bedroom

Mum and I
cleared out my room
to fill a bag for the charity shop.

Soft, cuddly teddies
on my bed.
Big and little dolls
I don't play with.
Messy bedroom!
Tiny pink jumper
a two-year-old size,
purple nightie.
Yuk! Yuk! Yuk!
Messy bedroom!
Little socks
grey and old
pink pyjamas - no!
Snakes and ladders game.
Messy bedroom!
Black, fluffy Mum dog
and her girl and boy puppies
stay with me.
I love them on my bed.

Harriet Harker (10)
Longdon St Mary's CE (VA) Primary School, Tewkesbury

The Compost Bin

I share a mud bed with my best friend Fred,
Squash!
It's a curly wurly world.
Tangle!
Someone's lifting up the lid, putting tea bags in.
Delicious!
Tea bags like shrivelled dates.

I'm squidgy and long, like spaghetti.
Wriggle!
I'm big, I'm bold and I'm blind.
Bump!
It's dark and wet, it's never cold.
Squelch!

I eat leaves like damp paper.
Dead flowers are dry as dust.
Paper as white as a cloud.
Grass cuttings like discarded hair.
Vegetable peelings, as light as a feather.
Banana skins like black strips of leather.

Can you guess what I am?
I'm a squashy, tangly, wriggly, squelchy worm.

Lizzie Fletcher (10)
Longdon St Mary's CE (VA) Primary School, Tewkesbury

A Light Bulb

I am a light bulb, as bright as the sun,
Once there was light and then there was none,
Now I can't have anymore fun.

I was thrown into a giant green bin,
There were lots of things like a bottle of gin,
There were lots of different bottles making a din.

Next I was tipped into a skip,
I guessed I was on another trip,
I wondered where I was going, maybe the tip?

The skip stopped at the recycling site,
I got sorted into a pile on the right,
Just then I got an almighty fright.

I was put into a nasty machine,
Which looked ferociously mean,
I was as still as a jelly bean.

The very next day I was a new one,
I am a light bulb as bright as the sun
Now I can have all of my fun.

Danielle Price (10)
Longdon St Mary's CE (VA) Primary School, Tewkesbury

Blue Tit

He has colourful, bright feathers
Blue as the clear blue sky
Bright as the yellow morning sun.

He's as small as a brown pine cone
Has little bouncy feet
He loves eating huge brown nuts
And for pudding slippery, slimy worms.

He's adorable, fuzzy and snuggly
He lives in a small twiggy nest
In a tall, leafy tree.

He soars like a gigantic plane
He's a lean mean flying machine,
He tweets all day long
Singing out his song.

Please! keep feeding the birds
So the species don't die out
All you have to feed them is nuts
Please! so we can hear their beautiful songs.

Ryan Jones (11)
Longdon St Mary's CE (VA) Primary School, Tewkesbury

My Thoughts

In my thoughts
I recognise the blustery wind knocking out the trees.
In my thoughts
I hear the rusty leaves drop to the ground.
In my thoughts
I scent the honey of the bees.
In my thoughts
I feel the scaly skin of a dragon.

Naylor Chambers (10)
Middleton Primary School, Wollaton Park

The Sea Sprite

I push the sea in and out with a whisk of my hand,
I stretch the slow sea across the land.

I grind the sand to make tiny grains
And pick up all the treasures before it rains.

I scatter the small sharp shells everywhere
And I shape the slippery, slimy seaweed with care.

I make the rocks fat and tall
And make the winds howl and call.

I make the salty taste in the air
And I make the caves and lairs.

I make it merry and fun,
I make it pleasant for everyone.

Megan Richmond (10)
Middleton Primary School, Wollaton Park

Creepy-Crawlies

A centipede requires a multitude of socks,
They keep their shoes in a cardboard box.

No house for spiders, just immense webs,
At night, while you're sleeping they join you in bed.

The ugly hornets make such a sound,
You hear them buzz when they hit the ground.

In the life of a bug, from a beetle to a slug,
Scary and hairy, slimy and snug.

Bryce-Lucas Scalia (10)
Middleton Primary School, Wollaton Park

Teachers

Teachers are nice,
Teachers are cool,
Teachers are sometimes boring,
But there is one teacher and he is the best
And that's my teacher.
He is a pest and better than all the rest,
He makes me laugh and drool,
He makes his lessons fun and cool,
He is a bit weird sometimes
Because he sings weird songs,
But I like that a lot,
Now do you see, he is the best
And better than all the rest.

Clare Saxton (10)
Middleton Primary School, Wollaton Park

What I Hate

I hate war
It makes me feel sore
And the terrifying sound
Of the bombs when they hit the ground.

I hate sadness
It makes me suffer madness
With the hateful sound of weeping
When children have trouble sleeping.

I hate pollution
I believe there's no solution
When people kill the ozone layer
I have to start saying my prayer.

Beth Marsden (9)
Middleton Primary School, Wollaton Park

In My Thoughts

In my thoughts a bird
Was gliding through the glittery sky.

In my thoughts I heard a horse
Go clickety-clack as the time went tick-tock.

In my thoughts an ogre strolled by
Through the field of sunflowers.

In my thoughts a bull charged
By the sandpit next to my garden.

Jasmine Shearsmith (10)
Middleton Primary School, Wollaton Park

Cornwall

I recognise the wind blowing
On the sailing boats floating away.

I watched the sun
Rising up into the sky.

I heard the roaring sea
The echo of people shouting
The splashing of water as they play.
The cars flying past and beeping.

I tasted chips, orange,
Sausage and kebab.

I feel the trees
As they sway and shake.

I smelt the chips with burger
And sausages with curry.
The sweet smell of candyfloss
With toffee apples.

I dream that I can go again
And stay there forever.

Aerran Dirs (10)
Middleton Primary School, Wollaton Park

The Dragon's 5 Wishes

I wish that I could stare straight at a great white shark
Hunt down its prey as quick as lightning.

I wish that I could hear the wolf's howl
As he bewares his prey as he comes to capture you.

I wish that I could touch the dragon's scaly back
As he sleeps in a deep slumber in his dark, dirty cave.

I never could wish for all of these wishes to be gone
Straight away from me as quick as that.

But I could always wish for freedom so that people won't slay me
Or capture me, that's my wish that I want to come true.

Jack Brown (10)
Middleton Primary School, Wollaton Park

Mum

She's the greatest,
No one can replace her
She's bright, pretty and intelligent.

Her smile lights her face,
Her hugs are better than the rest,
Her dinners are so delicious,
But the curries are the best!

If I behave my treat is sweets,
Don't get her mad,
For if you do, beware!

I could never live without her,
She does everything for me,
She loves me and I love her.

Mehreen Khan (9)
Middleton Primary School, Wollaton Park

Water Spirit

Waves ripple gently upon the shore,
Sand level rising, more, more
Shells washing up within the sand
Travelled far from a distant land
And the baby sleeps . . .

White horses galloping towards the rocks
Seagulls squawking, scattering flocks
Waves rising up, crests turn white
Tossing up fish in the stormy night . . .
And the baby sleeps . . .

Window ajar, in the starless night
Salty wind blowing with all its might
Pressing through the curtains, the bitter draught drives
But the baby knows of nothing, and silent she lies . . .
And she sleeps, sleeps.

Gale gives up, soaring low
Whispering a tune to the seabed below
Sea starts to rumble, sending ripples everywhere
White sea horses, transporting her with care
And the baby sleeps.

Through the great window, the dainty spirit drifts
And carefully up the baby she lifts
Haunting the victim's peaceful dreams
In a trance, the infant seems . . . but she sleeps.

Off, and into the echoing night
Now merely a distant turquoise light
Dipping and diving, far away
Time creeping on towards the hours of day
Shrieking and sobbing, the infant gives up,
Fallen deep into the ocean's dark cup.

Katie Kinnear (10)
Middleton Primary School, Wollaton Park

The Pea-Green Dragon

There's a story of an evil dragon
A story I know so well
And if you listen carefully
Then it's a story I will tell

It happened one cruel Monday
Near a filthy lake
(This story is so scary
It still makes me shake!)

There was a tiny girl
Sitting near some bracken
Then she turned around
And saw a gigantic dragon

It had scales of stunning green
It had eyes of fiery red
Smoke was pouring from its nose
And it had a gruesome head

The girl just stood there staring
Then drank from her plastic cup
But as soon as she swallowed,
The dragon gobbled her up

The dragon lived for years and years
Devouring all it saw
All it did was eat and eat
But still it wanted more

It brought misery to the world
Until one dreadful day
When a very heroic knight
Decided to start to slay

He crept up to the dragon
While it was soundly sleeping
But it had one eye open
It was really peeping!

Suddenly it breathed out fire
So the slayer got killed and burnt
The dragon didn't care one bit
'Well, that's his lesson learnt!'

It retired away to Scotland
And relaxed alone in a lake
That's what the Loch Ness monster is,
Not a big, fat snake!

Isobel Upjohn (9)
Middleton Primary School, Wollaton Park

The Arctic

Its bitter wind brushes along my face making everything shiver.
Everything white except a few specks of green
Like a white, deserted land
Except the animals that live there
Like a polar bear covered in soft, white fur,
An Arctic wolf running over the white horizon,
An Arctic hare burrowing down deep into the hillside
Covered in layers of chunky, broad white powdery snow.
Seals plunging deep into the gigantic turquoise ocean
Swimming and playing merrily.

Charlotte O'Leary (9)
Middleton Primary School, Wollaton Park

The Dragon Of All Dragons

It has razor-sharp claws
which can easily and powerfully swipe objects.
It has giant wings, beating at a fast but steady pace.
Such huge eyes, such scaly skin, far bigger than a dustbin.
It has enormous feet with big pointy nails
and a big, long tail slashing behind it.
Nothing on Earth can destroy it for this dragon is extremely strong.

Suleman Shamshad (9)
Middleton Primary School, Wollaton Park

Dirty Danny

Dirty Danny is a very dirty boy,
With mud all over like a messed up toy.
He digs down, down, deep, deep down,
Moving his legs and hands into the ground.
He finds a queen from chess, and a very old shoe,
An old music box and a dustbin too.
He lunges more downward until he finds treasure,
Just enough but more to measure.
He says, 'What shall I do with all this money?
Maybe I could go in a shop and buy honey!'
Then he goes up until he comes up to the top,
Leaves the garden and goes into a shop
And buys some chocolate and a bottle of pop.
The shopkeeper gives the change, and off goes Danny
With his pop and chocolate and lots more to carry.
He went inside and ate his food
And that's the adventure done in his mood!

William Moody (10)
Mill Lane Primary School, Chinnor

I Must Be Crazy

I woke up this morning, guess what I found?
A cow sitting in the lounge!
I looked in the bedroom, guess what I saw?
A big, fat boar!
I went to the kitchen and this is what I see?
Two baboons going barmy!
I went to the bathroom as I got in,
I noticed a penguin having a swim!
I went to the shed
And found a hippo dead.
I went to the attic, I saw two eyes
Then I got a big surprise.
A lion jumped out of the two eyes.
I went to the office, and guess what I saw?
A big snake just slithered past me.

Hannah Harvey (9)
Mill Lane Primary School, Chinnor

Squeak (My Cat)

He miaows and purrs,
Pounces and jumps.
He beats up my other cat
But that's Squeak for you.

He climbs up trees,
Pretends he's stuck.
Likes to attack birds
But that's Squeak for you.

He used to squeak when he was a kitten
That's how he got his name.
Sometimes I think he can talk
And that's Squeak for you.

Sophie Greenwood (9)
Mill Lane Primary School, Chinnor

The Dog In The Rain

The dog was sitting in the rain,
I bet he didn't have a name,
He woofed and barked,
He was parked,
In the little space,
Then started to lick my shoe lace,
So I took him home with me
And gave him a spot of tea,
He got into his snug little bed
And then snored off his little head!

Adam MacKerron (9)
Mill Lane Primary School, Chinnor

Bubbles

Bubbles are light,
Bubbles are pretty,
Bubbles are bright,
Bubbles in the city.

Bubbles are fun,
Bubbles are wet,
Bubbles in the sun,
Bubbles in a set.

Bubbles are nice,
Bubbles are shiny,
Bubbles are like ice,
Bubbles can be tiny.

Bubbles in the sky,
Bubbles near the ground,
Bubbles can go high,
Bubbles go round and round.

Samantha Bull (9)
Mill Lane Primary School, Chinnor

The Postbox

Monday morning, 9am,
The postman opens me up,
Puts his hands in like a cup,
He puts the letters in his van,
What a jolly happy postman.

Sitting there every day
The day is OK
But I still sit there rain or shine
But I don't whine.

Here I am, another day
The postman did not come yesterday,
I am nearly full,
Then I heard a call.

I'm missing him,
My life is getting dim,
Here comes a van,
It is the postman.

Connor Wheeler (10)
Mill Lane Primary School, Chinnor

Thomas Edison Fiction/Non-Fiction

Thomas Edison invented the light bulb,
What did he use for a mould?
The only problem was it kept melting down,
He probably acted like a clown!
He must have had a sigh and a moan,
Then he invented the telephone.
When he was putting up a border
He thought of the cylinder recorder.
Soon Thomas Edison was lying in a grave,
Do you think he had a shave'?

Peter Cooper (9)
Mill Lane Primary School, Chinnor

Envelope

I've been posted again,
I wonder who to, perhaps a lady or a man,
Can it be?
I wonder who I'll see?
Here comes the postman,
Come to collect me.
In the black sack I go,
Next to me was an envelope with a bow
And whoopee, I'm there, through I go,
To the mat.
A man with a tie picked me up
And opened me with care,
He rips me with a dare.
Inside me is a card,
He found some hard card,
On the card it had a note,
I think it's a bill!

Vicky Price (10)
Mill Lane Primary School, Chinnor

A Bubble

When you blow a bubble,
It doesn't make a sound,
It's never been in trouble,
It pops upon the ground.

When it floats in the sky all day,
The wind blows it around,
Children like to say hooray,
When it comes back down.

He likes to fly by the birds,
And over the sea,
People can't catch their words,
When they see he.

Ellen Higgs (10)
Mill Lane Primary School, Chinnor

A Snowflake

It flies around all day long,
Camouflaged in the snow,
People say the snow has gone,
But how do they know?

A snowflake is really cool,
Feeling cold all through the day,
Although it is really small,
It doesn't know the real way.

I think snowflakes are really pretty
And they're even better than a kitty.

Lucie Brand (10)
Mill Lane Primary School, Chinnor

My World

I was skipping along the winding stream,
Wondering what I would see
I sat down and had a dream
Suddenly I fell asleep

In my head I see, I see . . .

I see a football team
A man drinking tea
I hear the ripple of the sea
A lady swimming very deep

In my head I see, I see . . .

I see lots of steam
And a man paying his fee
I wake up and look at me
And roll down a hill and hear a beep

In my head that's what I see.

Lauren Bishop (10)
Mill Lane Primary School, Chinnor

The Elephant

It's wild and big, it's tall and sprout,
It runs around all about,
It's black and grey,
Sometimes I see him every day.

He's my very best friend,
In the whole wide world,
I know he's a wild animal,
But I don't care.

I know his name off by heart,
My big, big gorgie tart,
I know his tusks, I know his smell,
Sometimes it's weird as well.

He's getting old, he's getting tired,
I'm really worried,
I don't know what to do,
Just then he falls, the earth clatters,
I don't know what matters.

He's gone I know it, he's not coming back,
I'm just lying there, lying there with my big black hat,
And then I hear a noise,
But now I know I have to go,
My work is done,
With my best friend!

Abbie Bratt (10)
Mill Lane Primary School, Chinnor

Scrabble

She sits by herself,
Stuffing food into her cheeks.
She looks like a cloud,
Running round and round in her ball.

Her cheeks look like they have balls in,
But I know it's just food.
She likes food,
But she loves treats.

Every day she wakes up,
Eats and then just sleeps again
And every day I give her water
And give her food.

The first time I cleaned her out,
I lifted her up and she bit me
So I quickly let go of her
And Mum quickly put the top of the cage back on.

The second time we cleaned her out
Mum wore gardening gloves.
Mum took the top of the cage off.
Oh no, she's running away,
I found her ball and her in it.

Nicola Lawrence (9)
Mill Lane Primary School, Chinnor

Imaginary Friend

Imaginary friend, imaginary friend
No one has ever seen him.
He drives me around the bend,
He is like a floating fairy,
He stays right by me to play,
Hip hip hooray! Hip hip hooray!
Imaginary friend, imaginary friend
No one has ever seen him.
He drives me around the bend,
When all my friends are mean to me
He stays right by me and looks after me.
Imaginary friend, imaginary friend
No one has ever seen him.
He drives me around the bend,
No one can ever touch him,
He'll be with me till the end.

Sophie Diaper (10)
Oakfield Primary School, Totton

Love

Love is pink, like blossom falling from a tree.
It sounds like Mum and Dad having sloppy kisses.
It tastes like wafers and chocolate ice cream in a bowl.
It smells like strawberries and cream on a plate.
It looks like a crispy bar of chocolate.
It feels like a lovely big hug.
It reminds me of my great grandad.

Isobel Thompson (8)
Old Fletton Primary School, Peterborough

Fear

Fear is black like this pen.
It sounds like the dripping of a tap in a dungeon.
It tastes like a bird's tear.
It smells like dead bodies.
It feels like a stranger's hand on my back.
It reminds me of my dead grandad.

Shona Barrett (9)
Old Fletton Primary School, Peterborough

Sadness

Sadness sounds like a violin playing its saddest tune.
It tastes like bitter lemon and ice cola.
It smells like gone-off milk and dry pretzels.
It looks like a cold, damp hovel.
It feels like you've got the flu.
Sadness is blue, a sad colour.
It reminds me of snow.

Finola Murtagh (8)
Old Fletton Primary School, Peterborough

Love

Love is strawberry-red.
It sounds like Brian May playing his guitar.
It tastes like chicken legs.
It smells like Creme Eggs.
It looks like millions of volts.
It feels like a hot bath waiting for me.
It reminds me of Mr Davey and me playing the guitar.

Jordan Heather (8)
Old Fletton Primary School, Peterborough

Hate

Hate is blue, like rain pouring down my face.
It sounds like Michael Jackson screaming 'Wow!'
It tastes like mouldy raisins.
It smells like a mouldy lolly.
It looks like a brown, hairy mole.
It feels like dough in water.
It reminds me of my worst fight ever.

Natasha Petchey (9)
Old Fletton Primary School, Peterborough

Anger

Anger is like a black cloud.
It tastes like burnt toast.
It sounds like a stormy night.
It feels like a hot oven.
It looks like a snapping crocodile.
It smells like horrid smoke.
It reminds me of smashing things.

Hanna-Joe Cox (7)
Peartree Primary School, Welwyn Garden City

Sadness

Sadness is blue like the rain
It tastes like salt
It sounds like quiet music
It looks like saying goodbye.

Yilmaz Taycur (8)
Peartree Primary School, Welwyn Garden City

Snow

Today we went sledging
up in the snow,
high up in the mountains
the sun was aglow.

My sister went fast,
she did scream and yell,
we laughed and we laughed
until she fell.

Then we had a snowball fight
I won of course,
lots of snowballs and grass
Then I fell in the gorse.

George Williams (9)
Peniel CP School, Carmarthen

Griff

When I look out to the field
I just wonder if
My pony's there beneath the tree,
My pony's name is Griff.

He's 11 hands 2, he's all white,
And grazes all day long,
I think about him every day
When to school I've gone.

And when I go to bed I dream
And say a little prayer,
Next time I look out to the field,
My Griff will still be there.

Llywela Davies (10)
Peniel CP School, Carmarthen

My Farm

My name is Dafydd,
I live on a farm.
These are my animals
I keep out of harm.
Five chickens, two Jack Russells,
One sheepdog and one lurcher.

They say a dog is
A man's best friend.
This is very true so
Don't ask for a lend.
I won the sports
Because of my Jack Russell coach.

Foster the lurcher is the dog for me
He's beauty in motion when running free.

Dafydd Jones (10)
Peniel CP School, Carmarthen

The Long Walk

The oak trees tower over me,
Until the dark shadow is all I can see,
Do the trees scrape the sky?
Are they taller than an eagle can fly?
Now it is becoming night,
With not a flicker or sound or light,
And then the trees part,
And with a sudden beat of my heart,
I see the stars dance away,
Until it is at last time for day.

Matthew Edward Kilgariff (11)
Peniel CP School, Carmarthen

My Pets

I have five pets
Which run up big debts,
It's not just the food, it's not just the bedding,
It's the things they wreck, it's doing my head in!

The camera chip was eaten by Noddy,
Destroyed the photos of Christmas and everybody.

My cute little hamster chewed through a wire,
I didn't worry till the telly went on fire!

Tom the cat was chasing a bat,
He thought he could fly, he had a good try,
He crashed down on the iron, on the carpet it fell,
It burnt a huge hole, made a terrible smell.

The guinea pig, Holly, was left out to roam,
She liked to explore all around her new home,
She thought that her toilet was the computer keyboard,
Something went *bang* and how my dad roared!

Smudge is the oldest and tries hard to please,
But she gives such a welcome, she scratches your knees.

My pets are a hassle and all the mischief they cause,
But what would my house be without claws and paws?
They're part of the family, they cheer us all up,
Next Christmas I'll ask for a St Bernard pup!

Bethan Cumber (9)
Peniel CP School, Carmarthen

The Seasons

As wintertime draws to a close,
I think of the seasons gone by.
Autumn with its hue of colours,
Bright stars in a clear black sky.

Then winter with Christmas,
Perhaps the most special time of all.
Even more exciting
If the snow should start to fall!

But for my mum,
Spring has to be the best!
With snowdrops opening
And birds in the nest.

Hooray for summer,
Warm days by the sea!
Sunshine and laughter
With friends and family.

Claudia Jones (9)
Peniel CP School, Carmarthen

The Best Book Ever

I once took a book out of school
and when I started reading, it was very cool.
I read a bit more day by day,
and I couldn't stop reading it, I must say.
There I stood, there I lay
reading and reading every day.
But when it was time to take the book back,
I missed it a lot but that was that.

Amelia Cox (10)
Peniel CP School, Carmarthen

I Like School

I like school
because it's cool,
I like school
because I'm no fool.
I like school because you see,
the teachers are good
and they teach me.

Robert Jones (10)
Peniel CP School, Carmarthen

What Is Red?

Red is a red, red rose standing nice and tall,
Red is my hairbands tied up in my hair,
Red is fire, hot and fierce,
Sometimes red is the colour of my socks,
Red is the colour of my pencil case,
Red is the colour of strawberries in my fruit bowl,
Red is a poppy in a meadow.

Tammie Leigh Sinnott (9)
Portway Junior School, Andover

What Is Yellow?

Yellow is the bus on a sunny school morning?
Sometimes yellow is my teacher's magnets,
Yellow is my homework diary, all scruffy and old,
Yellow paper so crumpled and crushed,
Yellow is the sun so fiery and bright,
Yellow number line on the wall so long and sleek,
Yellow is the canoe on that sunny fishing trip,
Yellow is the daffodils out in the garden.

Ben Biddlecombe (9)
Portway Junior School, Andover

What Is Red?

Red is blood, red is warning,
Sometimes red is red, red paint,
Red is signs that tell you to stop,
Red is anger that streams through your head,
Sometimes red is that bad devil,
And red is that feeling you get inside
And want to hide.
Red is part of the union flag,
And of course, red is royalty,
Red is roses on Valentine's Day,
Red is sweets
And always lipstick!

Georgie Wheldon (9)
Portway Junior School, Andover

What Is Blue?

B lue is a colour of a rainbow,
L ight and dark the colour can be,
U tterly a boring colour for me but is an
E ndless colour of the sea.

Elle-Louise Heard (9)
Portway Junior School, Andover

What Is Green?

Green is blades of grass in a field,
Green is a caterpillar crawling up a stem,
Green is the stem of a flower,
Green reminds me of leaves on a tree.

Jack Short (8)
Portway Junior School, Andover

What Is Black?

Black is the colour of tiger stripes,
And the thick black hair that belongs to a witch,
Black is a colour that keeps people away,
At least until another day.
Black is the colour that everyone dreads,
Sometimes black really gets into your head.
Black is the colour of a witch's cloak,
That sweeps behind her like a puff of smoke.
Black is the colour of a killer whale,
That has a great, big, splashing tail.
Black is a very evil colour,
But you need it to live, there is no doubt about it.

Eleanor Roche (9)
Portway Junior School, Andover

What Is Green?

Sometimes green is paint,
big and bold.

Green is the blades of grass
in my back garden.

Green is paper being cut.

Sometimes green is a soft carpet,
green is the colour of a helpful file.
Can you imagine living without it?

Flinn Kenward (8)
Portway Junior School, Andover

What Is Blue?

Blue is the colour of the deep, dark sea,
Blue is the dolphins gliding about in the ocean waves,
Blue reminds me of the sky on a summer's day,
Blue reminds me of my paper I colour with at home,
Blue is a colour in the rainbow,
Blue reminds me of my pen I write with at school,
Blue is the colour of butterflies fluttering about on a summer's day,
Blue reminds me of my school uniform,
Blue reminds me of whales splashing about on the surface,
Blue reminds me of sea horses swimming about in the reef.

Laura Jones (8)
Portway Junior School, Andover

What Is Red?

Red is nasty blood coming out of my body,
Sometimes red is the colour of flowers in my garden,
Red reminds me of Liverpool football team,
Sometimes red reminds me of scoring a goal in football,
Red is a sparkling car zooming along in the rain,
Red is the sunset as I go to bed.

Daniel Andrews (8)
Portway Junior School, Andover

What Is Red?

Red is the sun rising in the morning sky,
Red is the blood squirting out of your hand,
Red is the beautiful roses in your garden,
Red is the small rubber ball that you play with,
Red is the boxing gloves that you fight with,
Red is the comments in my books made by my teacher,
Red is the sunset going down at the end of the day.

Matthew Jenkins (9)
Portway Junior School, Andover

What Is Black?

Black is a rose,
Sometimes ink is black,
Black is a jumper I wear,
Sometimes black is spiders crawling around,
Black is ashes from a fire,
Black is cars going by,
Sometimes my coats are black,
Oil is black, very black,
Black is mud on the floor,
Black is my shoe polish,
Sometimes you are black from coming down a chimney,
Black is the colour of cats' fur.

Adam North (8)
Portway Junior School, Andover

What Is Purple?

Purple is the colour of my bedroom walls
Gleaming in the light,
Purple reminds me of my bed cover
Keeping me warm in the night,
Purple is the colour of flowers
That are open till the midnight hours.
Purple is an octopus
Waiting to eat fish,
Purple is the colour of paint
Waiting to go on the walls,
Purple is my favourite colour
And soon it will be yours!

Abigail Portsmouth (8)
Portway Junior School, Andover

What Is Blue?

Blue reminds me of my fountain pen when I am working very hard,
Blue is the colour of thunder and lightning in the dark night sky,
Blue reminds me of my school jumper, comfortable and soft.
Sometimes blue is the colour of the sky as the clouds pass by.

Chloe Rowland (8)
Portway Junior School, Andover

Bear

Inside the bear's fur, the warmth of the sun,
Inside the warmth of the sun, the bear's heart,
Inside the bear's heart, the black hole,
Inside the black hole, the bear's eyes,
Inside the bear's eyes, a bright star,
Inside the bright star, the bear's claw,
Inside the bear's claw, the pain of a dying animal,
Inside the pain of a dying animal, the bear's fang,
Inside the bear's fang, a stormy blizzard,
Inside the stormy blizzard, the bear's fur.

Sam Beecroft (10)
Portway Junior School, Andover

What Is Black?

Black are my clothes,
Black is my hair,
Black is my pen on paper
And the headphones in my CD player,
Sometimes black is like a spider.
What does black remind you of?

Jamie Barry (9)
Portway Junior School, Andover

Witches' Spell
(Inspired by Macbeth)

Fillet of a whale's flubber,
Leopards' spots and tigers' stripes,
The scorpion's poison and hair of a ghost,
That will make it for its most.

*'Double, double, toil and trouble,
Fire burn and cauldron bubble.'*

Next you add something very special,
The tail of a cat and fin of a dolphin,
The skin of a snake and fur of a dog,
That will make it for its best.

*'Double, double, toil and trouble,
Fire burn and cauldron bubble.'*

Jessica Allmark (9)
Portway Junior School, Andover

What Is A . . . Tidal Wave?

A tidal wave is a sink full of water
washing the dirt away.

A tidal wave is a million raindrops
falling down at once.

A tidal wave is a deep blue sky,
washing the clouds away.

A tidal wave is the colour blue in a rainbow,
diving down from the sky.

A tidal wave is a piece of blue paper,
with lots of little dots swimming in it.

Natasha Byrne (11)
St Edmund's CE Primary School, Mansfield Woodhouse

Buck And Chuck

Buck and Chuck are two tramps singing to you and me,
They are two little fluffy pillows,
They are sacks of potatoes dancing in a shed,
They are two guitars playing together,
Buck and Chuck are a white and red hat boogieing like fire.

Kelly Burbanks (11)
St Edmund's CE Primary School, Mansfield Woodhouse

On The Beach

Lots of children in the sun,
Having lots of wonderful fun,
Feeling the sand in their feet,
Sitting there in the heat.

Running out into the sea,
While shouting out with glee,
Sitting down on the sand,
The baby's holding Mummy's hand.

Putting on suncream,
While being hit by a sunbeam,
Children wearing flip-flops,
Also eating ice pops.

The fishes are swimming all around,
The children watching, not making a sound,
Suddenly the silence breaks, 'Look what I've found!'
Says Sally being a hound.

Kelsay Higton (10)
St Edmund's CE Primary School, Mansfield Woodhouse

The Iron Woman

T he Iron Woman,
H ere she was standing near the muddy marsh,
E verything around was so muddy.

I ron she was so metal,
R ising out of the muddy marsh,
O n the marsh Lucy met The Iron Woman,
N ear the marsh, she listened carefully.

W hen she got out of the marsh, she was dripping with mud,
O ne morning she woke up because it was light,
M any people met The Iron Woman,
A nd then Lucy went back to the castle,
N ever, but then The Iron Woman went to Lucy.

Stacey Redfern (10)
St Edmund's CE Primary School, Mansfield Woodhouse

The Iron Woman

T he marsh is sticky and full of weeds,
H ere she stands, a wash she needs,
E verything around is dirty and disgusting,

I ron she is made of, underneath the weeds she is shining.
R ising up ahead is the sun,
O n Lucy's driveway, The Iron Woman is the only one,
N ear is Lucy to give her a clean,

W hat kind of giant had she seen?
O f course it was light because it was morning,
M any people were driving past and staring,
A bout that time, Lucy's dad was at the factory,
N ow I'll leave you to think of the rest of the story.

Brooke Jephson (10)
St Edmund's CE Primary School, Mansfield Woodhouse

The Iron Woman

T he Iron Woman is her name,
H urt by the polluted water,
E els and fishes suffering with the pain.

I s there anything we can do?
R ubbish destroying all of nature,
O ozing onto the seas and oceans wide,
N obody caring what damage is left behind.

W oman of iron, what can you do?
O tters and animals getting killed too,
M ake them see what they are doing,
A ll the countryside they are destroying.
N ations' waste is contaminating all.

Sorel O'Berg (10)
St Edmund's CE Primary School, Mansfield Woodhouse

The Iron Woman

T he Iron Woman's eyes were hurting,
H ow do we stop her?
E ither we can get the hose out.

I ron Woman,
R ope of a hosepipe,
O n the muddy footstep
N othing will work properly.

W ill we stop?
O n the horizon in 10 minutes,
M onstrous, look very angry,
A lways looks angry,
N othing looks like her.

Martin North (10)
St Edmund's CE Primary School, Mansfield Woodhouse

The Iron Woman

T he huge Iron Woman arises from the muddy marsh,
H eavy with mud, full of rage and hate,
E ven against her own kind.

I t is so sad,
R ather fight with the whole world,
O r so it seems from my eyes,
N ever to have the love of a family.

W e all need to keep the peace,
O r what a world to live in,
M ankind might not want to keep the peace,
A nimals might die and so might I!
N ot if we all try.

Anthony Glynne-Jones (10)
St Edmund's CE Primary School, Mansfield Woodhouse

The Iron Woman

T he Iron Woman felt the water burning her eyes,
H er finger and thumb picked up Lucy,
E veryone thought the birdwatcher was mad.

I t was amazing how big The Iron Woman was,
R ound in circles went the eel,
O h no, the screaming was too much for Lucy,
N ow she tried to break free.

W hen everyone was asleep, The Iron Woman came to see Lucy,
O ver the fields she ran and into the river,
M any a time The Iron Woman came up for air,
A nd she too began to rub her eyes.
'N ow you're clean,' said Lucy.

Ethan Brown (10)
St Edmund's CE Primary School, Mansfield Woodhouse

The Iron Woman

T he Iron Woman can smell the fear from the sea,
H er eyes are red like balls of fire,
E els are dying from the pollution in the sea.

I can see The Iron Woman in tears and her eyes sad,
R opes of hosepipes to clean The Iron Woman.
O n Lucy's driveway The Iron Woman taps at her window,
N ow Lucy wakes and sees The Iron Woman in anger.

W ater from the sea is going all dirty from pollution,
O n Lucy's window, Lucy climbs down The Iron Woman's body,
M etal on The Iron Woman's body gets all cold,
A whale is dying from the pollution,
N ow Lucy and The Iron Woman can hear the pain from all the animals.

Tia Read (10)
St Edmund's CE Primary School, Mansfield Woodhouse

The Iron Woman

T all as a tree
H inges in the body
E ntertaining.

I tsy bitsy heart
R age like fire
O range hair
N aughty.

W et iron
O minous stare
M essy
A lice is her name
N oisy.

Alice Sentance (10)
St Edmund's CE Primary School, Mansfield Woodhouse

The Iron Woman

T he Iron Woman Is angry
H er hair is made from wires
E very day she gets angrier and angrier

I ron Woman is made from metal
R ound the city The Iron Woman goes to get to Lucy's house
O n the river that has been polluted The Iron Woman goes crazy
N ow that the factory has polluted The Iron Woman wants to
                              burn down the factory

W omen scream as they see The Iron Woman
O beyed Lucy
M en shout as The Iron Woman comes
A ll the eyes of The Iron Woman have tears in them
N ow that the river is polluted the animals are crazy.

Coral Booth (10)
St Edmund's CE Primary School, Mansfield Woodhouse

The Iron Woman

T he Iron Woman
H er legs are grey and long
E yes black and red

I ce-cold hands
R ound head
O nly just out of the water
N ew and just clean

W alks with heavy legs
O ut of all the pollution
M ad about the factories
A nd can hear the fish and things that are hurt
N ice to Lucy.

Emily Minett (10)
St Edmund's CE Primary School, Mansfield Woodhouse

The Iron Woman

T he Iron Woman could smell the mud dripping off her.
H aving seen the photographer trying to get her on his lens
E ye-witnessing the whole event he saw The Iron Woman.

I ntending to photograph The Iron Woman
R unning, trying to get away from her
O n and on as he ran, The Iron Woman throwing mud
N early reached the muddy marsh, the mud dripping off her.

W hen she gets back to the muddy marsh she feels the iron
O n the marsh when she gets angry her eyes turn red
M ud still dripping off into the marsh
A nd then the photographer still walking home, mud on him
N owhere to be seen, The Iron Woman in the muddy marsh.

Chelsey Nicholls (10)
St Edmund's CE Primary School, Mansfield Woodhouse

The Iron Woman

T he Iron Woman is so dirty as she rises out of the river
H ypnotised felt Lucy as she walked across the bridge
E asily annoyed, more than anyone else in the world

I n coming of the monster, Lucy runs
R unning as fast as she could
O h dear, thought the birdwatcher
N othing could be wrong, Lucy thought.

W oman, the bird watcher thought
O n her way, Lucy went home
M assive, huge
A mazing but horror
N othing she could do.

Billy Simpkin (10)
St Edmund's CE Primary School, Mansfield Woodhouse

Cat Rap

Cats are cool and they know it
Nothing ever seems to fit!
Cats are cool and you know it
Everybody shout out *cats!*

Cats are stupid, pretty and fat
Everybody likes a big fat cat!
Cats are stupid, pretty and fat
Everybody shout out *cats!*

Some cats have chubby legs and some don't
They want water, no they don't!
Some cats have chubby legs and some don't
Everybody shout out *cats!*

Cats go to sleep in blue night
Sometimes cats have a big fright!
Cats go to sleep in blue night
Everybody shout out *cats!*

Chloe Seddon (8)
St Edmund's CE Primary School, Mansfield Woodhouse

A Football Is . . .

A football is a person on a trampoline bouncing in the air
A football is a rainbow, all different colours
A football is a plane flying through the air
A football is a boxing bag because they get hit hard
A football is a planet floating around the world
A football is a spear heading for the goal!
A football is an arrow darting through the air
A football is a toilet roll rolling across the floor.

Kristian Pye (11)
St Edmund's CE Primary School, Mansfield Woodhouse

The Sun In The Summertime

The sun is a great ball of fire, burning in the sky
while shining on people's soft and gentle skin.
After the rain has been, the sun comes along
and softens the flower beds to make the flowers grow strong and tall.

Summertime is where the sun shines in the day
but on the other side of the Earth is darkness.

Meanwhile in the desert the sun is scorching hot
and makes the sand burn.
The sand is like fire burning on the bottom of your feet.

Natalie Mauri (11)
St Edmund's CE Primary School, Mansfield Woodhouse

The Iron Woman

T he Iron Woman is strong and made of metal
H ere she is strong as she can be
E ating all the seaweed.

I am the strongest in the land
R oaming everywhere in the sea
O n and on she goes, looking for Lucy
N o one knows where she is.

W atching all of the birds fly by
O n she searches round and round
M aybe she is looking for Lucy
A big-nosed monster
N ever giving up to protect the world.

Jessica Beresford (10)
St Edmund's CE Primary School, Mansfield Woodhouse

The Iron Woman

T he Iron Woman's hair is tangly
H er hair is made up from bits of tangled wire
E very part of her is polluted by the factory.

I rregular. The Iron Woman is irregular
R acket. The Iron Woman passed on a racket to Lucy
O utrageous. The Iron Woman is outrageous
N ice. The Iron Woman is nice to Lucy.

W ashed. The Iron Woman wanted the river to be washed
O beyed. The Iron Woman obeyed Lucy and they went to the canal
M achinery. The Iron Woman is made up of machinery
A bandoned. The Iron Woman was abandoned
N asty. The Iron Woman felt nasty about the factory people
                                         polluting the water.

Kia Martin (10)
St Edmund's CE Primary School, Mansfield Woodhouse

The Iron Woman

T he Iron Woman is a metal robot machine,
H er hand put a snowdrop on Lucy's window,
E verybody's drinking water has been polluted.

I n her hand she sees Lucy,
R obots are very good and do your jobs,
O n the other side she sees The Iron Woman covered in mud,
N obody likes the horrible Iron Woman.

W hy does The Iron Woman have to destroy my dad's factory?
O n her dad's factory are bits that have fallen off.
M y dad and me have a sad life,
A ll the time we will be miserable,
N ever see the factory again.

Kristie Richardson (10)
St Edmund's CE Primary School, Mansfield Woodhouse

A Window

A window is a mirror,
Reflecting your image.

A window is an icy waterfall,
Crashing from a cliff.

A window is a shield,
A shield from outside.

A window is a sheet of paper,
Shimmering in the sun.

A window is a magnifying glass,
Viewing small things.

Joshua Wardle (10)
St Edmund's CE Primary School, Mansfield Woodhouse

Aliens, Aliens

Aliens, aliens get on a bus
Aliens, aliens fall on Toys R Us
Aliens, aliens you are great
Aliens, aliens have you just ate?

Aliens, aliens you are cool
Aliens, aliens do you wanna play pool?
Aliens, aliens what is your name?
Aliens, aliens how about a game?

Aliens, aliens please tell me
Aliens, aliens have you been to Dundee?
Aliens, aliens can you swim?
Aliens, aliens I think you're a bit dim.

Aliens, aliens send me home
Aliens, aliens don't send me to the Millennium Dome
Aliens, aliens please help me
Aliens, aliens I'll pay you 10p!

Rebecca Lounds (9)
St Edmund's CE Primary School, Mansfield Woodhouse

River Maun

R ivers always lead into the sea
I t always makes me smile when I look at the green valley
V alleys always surround the River Maun
E ven when it is foggy
R iver banks always go down and slant into the water
                                              so it doesn't flood.

Zak Wycherley (9)
St Edmund's CE Primary School, Mansfield Woodhouse

School

School's where we see our mate
But some of us hate
School
School's where we learn and listen and play
We do this all day!
It's school, it's school, *it's school.*

We have assemblies which are great
Which some of us don't hear because we're late
For school
School's where we learn and listen and play
We do this all day!
It's school, it's school, *it's school.*

Children's teachers are really nice
And they're really precise
At school,
School's where we learn and listen and play
We do this all day!
It's school, it's school, *it's school.*

Sophie Mason (8)
St Edmund's CE Primary School, Mansfield Woodhouse

Winning The Cup

This is the man that scored the goal.

This is the man that scored the goal
That won the cup.

This is the man that scored the goal
That won the cup
For our home team.

This is the man that scored the goal
That won the cup
For our home team
And sent the crowd mad.

This is the man that scored the goal
That won the cup
For our home team
And sent the crowd mad
He brought the cup here for the first time ever.

Ben Jones (9)
St Edmund's CE Primary School, Mansfield Woodhouse

What Is A Blizzard?

A blizzard is as cold as a freezer,
A blizzard is a crying baby,
A blizzard is a bully pushing you to the ground.
A blizzard is the anger of God,
A blizzard snows people inside,
A blizzard is you eating an ice cream in the winter.

Jade Clay (10)
St Edmund's CE Primary School, Mansfield Woodhouse

The River Maun

The River Maun glistens like stars at night,
splashing round the corners turning left and right.
Happy people walking their dogs,
being careful not to stand on mice or frogs.

The River Maun is like small, shiny gems,
but it's not as long as the River Thames.
Children paddling in the river,
even in the cold with a great big shiver.

The River Maun is like a piece of glass,
laid next to a line of grass.
The moles come out at night
and give dog walkers a terrible fright.

The River Maun is like the moon above,
the kind that all the fish love.
Children love to feed the ducks
and everyone loves the way the river looks.

Stacey Hill (10)
St Edmund's CE Primary School, Mansfield Woodhouse

Rippling River

R unning, rippling river
I n a meadow
V ery fast and furious
E normous fields
R ippling, running river.

Ashley McMillan (9)
St Edmund's CE Primary School, Mansfield Woodhouse

The River Maun

T he thick, tall trees stand alone
H eavy rocks all around
E legant scenery there to stay.

R obin redbreast flutters by
I cy cold water in the winter
V icious ripples of water float along
E verlasting land
R iver flowing by.

M any fish swimming by the rocks
A pples blossom on the trees
U nder the bridge the river stands
N ight-time isn't far away so that is for today.

April Shannon (9)
St Edmund's CE Primary School, Mansfield Woodhouse

The River Maun

T errific river
H uge river
E normous, sparkling river

R acing, very fast river
I n the river are some rocks
V icious river
E very day meanders
R ippling river

M eadowy river
A gusty river
U nder the river it is misty
N ear the river is a muddy bank.

Chloe Jevons (9)
St Edmund's CE Primary School, Mansfield Woodhouse

The River Maun

T he River Maun
H ow it flows
E verlasting.

R iver valleys
I t is so powerful
V iew its flow
E very week I go to it
R ivers are great.

M y dad goes there
A nd I do too
U ndoubtedly a beautiful place
N ever forget it.

Michael Wallis (9)
St Edmund's CE Primary School, Mansfield Woodhouse

The River Maun

R ivers always meander
I ncluding streams
V icious water flows
E verybody visits the River Maun
R ain from the sky flows into the River Maun

M any people visit the River Maun
A ll sorts of people love it
U nusual objects appear in the River Maun
N ot many people hate the River Maun.

Adam Gallagher (9)
St Edmund's CE Primary School, Mansfield Woodhouse

The River Maun

T he river is surrounded by a green meadow
H ills are in the background of the River Maun
E veryone looked at the river in our class.

R iver ripples down until it ends
I t was a very nice day at the River Maun
V ehicles went on top of the River Maun
E veryone had to draw a picture of the River Maun
R iver Maun runs through Mansfield Woodhouse.

M any people take their dogs for a walk around the River Maun
A bridge goes across the river
U sually children play next to the river
N ow I know all about the *River Maun!*

Annabelle Cassidy (10)
St Edmund's CE Primary School, Mansfield Woodhouse

The River Maun

T he River Maun
H eather grows nearby
E arthy banks.

R abbits are cute
I see fish
V ery cold water
E very day it is changing
R unning water over the rocks.

M any bushes to be seen
A nts are everywhere
U mbrellas are left on the bridge
N ature trails are to be found.

Daniel Hardwick (9)
St Edmund's CE Primary School, Mansfield Woodhouse

That's The Honest Truth
(Based on 'Word Of A Lie' by Jackie Ray)

I am the greatest footballer and
> *That's the honest truth.*

I am the strongest man and
> *That's the honest truth.*

I am the best Olympic runner and
> *That's the honest truth.*

I play for Manchester United and
> *That's the honest truth.*

I've got super powers and
> *That's the honest truth.*

I've got a talking dog and
> *That's the honest truth.*

I swam across the Atlantic Ocean and
> *That's the honest truth.*

I ate seven swords and
> *That's the honest truth.*

I can turn into a cartoon character and
> *That's the honest truth.*

I own a Ferrari Enzo and
> *That's the honest truth.*

I lie the most in our school and
> *That's the honest truth.*

Lewis Jephson (9)
St Edmund's CE Primary School, Mansfield Woodhouse

River

R ainwater makes the river bigger
I think the river sparkles in the sunlight
V icious rivers are called rapids
E verything about river is to do with water
R ivers flow and sparkle down the muddy banks.

Katie Rose (10)
St Edmund's CE Primary School, Mansfield Woodhouse

River

R iver's current comes down fast with a gust.
I t's been foggy and spooky for the last mysterious days.
V alleys covered in lush green grass.
E very tree branch swaying in the wind.
R olling water down the sparkling waterfall.

Ricky Blakey (9)
St Edmund's CE Primary School, Mansfield Woodhouse

Inside A Pirate's Pocket

A golden telescope
A treasure map
A bottle of poison
A battered cat
A shiny key
A skull of a human
And Peter Pan's knife
The enchanted rose
Slime of squid
Not forgetting a sharpener
Brain of dolphin
A ruby ring
And the magic wand
Cinderella's slipper
Sleeping Beauty's crown
Ariel's voice inside a shell
Rapunzel's hair
The king's crown
Jasmine's tiger
And a gun!

Leanne Greasley (9)
St James' CE (Aided) Junior School, Derby

Things You Find In A Pop Star's Pocket

A microphone you can speak through
A sequin off their clothes
Some headphones to listen to music
A book of signatures
A mobile phone
A camera to take photos
A chewy gum all soggy and wet
A little box of hair gel
A comb to brush their hair
A pen to write with
Glasses to wear
Now there's nothing left but a great big *hole!*

Tanzeela Hanif (9)
St James' CE (Aided) Junior School, Derby

Things In A Pirate's Pocket

A litre of sea
A small green pea
An eye patch
That he had snatched.

A postcard from his wife
A sharp and pointy knife
A parrot that can't squawk
A bent and broken fork.

All these things were in his pocket
But I think they've got lost
But they didn't cost very much.

Attiyah Riaz (8)
St James' CE (Aided) Junior School, Derby

I Know But You Don't

I know what a pop star has in her pocket
They have some lipstick if they are a girl
They walk around thinking they're it
But I know I'm prettier, don't you think?
They have some disgusting eyeliner,
Nail varnish and you know all that.
It's just ruining your face.
I know what I have in my pocket
I have joy and happiness
Because you see, you can't put happiness
And joy in your pocket,
You have to put it higher -
In your heart.

Somera Hussain (9)
St James' CE (Aided) Junior School, Derby

What's In a Pop Star's Pocket

A microphone you can speak through
A book of pictures to sign
An ear plug to hear the musical director
A CD player to hear songs
A comb to brush her hair
A box of make-up
A little box of hair gel
A pen to write with
A rose from the audience
A camera to take photos
A mobile phone to ring friends.
There is nothing now because
There was a big hole.

Miriam Khan (9)
St James' CE (Aided) Junior School, Derby

In A Pirate's Pocket

In a pirate's pocket there is:
A telescope to see,
An old map that marks the road to hot Hawaii,
A battered up and manky quill,
A piece of parchment,
A rat that is quite ill,
A pen that is very bent,
A rat that has just been born,
A tatty fish bone that is quite worn
And a bottle of beer,
A bottle of beer,
That's called *Morning Fear!*

Gwyneth Mabo (9)
St James' CE (Aided) Junior School, Derby

Why?

Crying, crying, crying
Sighing, sighing, sighing
People feeling sad
From the bullies who are mad.

Why, why, why
Why do they make me unhappy?
Why do they make me sad?
All I want is to be glad.

Tell someone!
About this depressing time
Don't keep it locked up inside
Where only you have the key.

Tell someone!
Or you will never be left alone
From these people
Who do not know how to be kind.

Nazneen Bamji (11)
St Patrick's RC Primary School, Grangetown

How Can Anyone Do This To Me?

How can anyone do this to me?
Punch me, kick me, push me, trip me
Why would anyone do this to me?
Call me names, throw things at me
How can anyone do this to me?

How can anyone do this to me?
I'm afraid of going to school
Walking alone, feeling unappreciated
Why would anyone do this to me?
I feel sad and isolated
I'm afraid to tell anyone
How can anyone do this to me?

How can anyone do this to me?
That's it!
I am going to tell *today*
Tell, tell, tell *every day*
Why would anyone do this to me?
'It's not your fault,' says the teacher,
'Always tell, don't let them win.'
How could I let anyone do this to me?

Niall Boyce (11)
St Patrick's RC Primary School, Grangetown

What Bullies Do

The person they are bullying doesn't find this pleasing.
Some people get bullied but don't complain.
There are people that enjoy giving pain.
Their feelings make them choose which one
They pick to torment, and the rest they will shun.
They do their routine name calling and teasing.

Dionne Scarico (10)
St Patrick's RC Primary School, Grangetown

Bullying

Bullying is horrible, I should know,
You feel down, sad and lonely and really, really low.
Outside you're OK, but inside it hurts,
Bullies could tease people about having a growth spurt!
What you feel is depression and you're very sad,
But . . . don't worry, they're not so hard!
Bullies think it's clever to bully, but it's not,
So, if you're being bullied, *tell the bully to stop!*

Being picked on for no reason is awful and bad,
Or even being called a name,
Or even saying something about your mum or your dad!
If a bully is taunting you in some way,
Tell a teacher, and then they'll pay!
If a bully has injured you,
It's only because they've got nothing else better to do,
Because . . . if you don't tell anyone, you feel suicidal . . .
And that is why . . .
The most important thing to do is to tell someone -
If you're being bullied.

Chloe Pride (11)
St Patrick's RC Primary School, Grangetown

Charlotte Church

Charlotte Church is her name
She is a famous Welsh singer
She walks around with her body full of fame
People pay me to give them a poster.

The Millennium Stadium is her thing
She sings there all the time
One day she watched Neil Jenkins play on the wing
He is really good, have you seen him play?

She lives in Cardiff Bay
In a penthouse at the very top
1st March is the best of her life.

Kirsty Nash (11)
St Patrick's RC Primary School, Grangetown

You And Me

You are you and I am me, we're as different as can be,
But that's no reason to pick on me!

You are big and I am small,
But with your help I could stand tall!

You are black and I am white,
But we don't always need to fight!

Every day you make me scared,
It's not like you're being dared!

Together we could have some fun,
But every day you make me run!

We don't need to fight this way,
We could be friends every day!

Come on don't be a bully,
Be kind and helpful just like me!

Michael Harrington (11)
St Patrick's RC Primary School, Grangetown

Bullying Is Bad!

Bullying is sad
It's like you're the only book left,
Bullying is bad
It makes you cry.

Bullying is unkind
It makes you mad,
Whenever you're sad
Tell someone.

Bullying is name calling,
But if you turn
Into a bully
Tell your mind to stop.

If you have been bullied
Tell someone!

Lauren Green (10)
St Patrick's RC Primary School, Grangetown

Bullies

Bullies, bullies are everywhere
Waiting for someone to scare
They hide to get you after school
To make you look such a fool
People watch afraid to butt in
For fear the next day it could be him.

Bullies pick on you in their gangs
That's the only way
One to one just wouldn't pay.

Bullies think they're hard
But they're not
Find them on their own
They would lose the plot.

Stamp them out once and for all
It's just a matter of time
They're heading for a fall.

Bullying happens!

Hannah Phillips (10)
St Patrick's RC Primary School, Grangetown

Catherine Jenkins

Wales and England playing a match
Catherine Jenkins walked onto the stage,
The crowd went silent
She started to sing.

A couple of voices seen not heard
Catherine doing a duet,
She sounds better on her own
That's what I think.

She stopped singing
The noise went back up again,
Catherine Jenkins the singer
The best I'll ever see.

Shanice Nicholls (11)
St Patrick's RC Primary School, Grangetown

Full Stop To Bullying!

Bullying is not very nice
Bullying is not right.
I think bullies should be stopped.
Everyone should watch, watch, watch.
Bullies can be stopped if someone tells on them.
Don't let them get away with it
So all you bullies out there beware
Because you're being watched
And you will be stopped
It would be good to have no bullies
And with a little help from everyone
We can help to stop bullies in their tracks
And stamp them out full stop!

Rachael Fanning (10)
St Patrick's RC Primary School, Grangetown

Pure Nature Is The Truth

A soft and gentle pansy,
Watching it grow,
Blending colours,
A tint of rose,
Purple explosion,
Sticky and brave,
Fireworks fired
And flowers remain,
Gerbera, pink velvet,
Layered hair,
Sun like a body,
A glimpse of air, multicoloured,
Golden jewels,
Nature calls,
Forget-me-not.

Jessica Elliott (11)
St Peter & St Paul Primary School, Bexhill-on-Sea

The Football Player

There was a man called Dean
The best player to be seen
The way he weaved around the park
We always knew he'd make his mark
Even from his days at Crewe
His super skills we all knew
First game at home he scored a goal
Now he's a hero to us all
And now he's bound to keep us up
And next year we are sure to win the cup
He has very good agility
There's no doubt about his ability
He is our record signing
With the position we're in it's perfect timing
That player Dean is purely the best
He gives defenders a real test!

Callum Thomas (9)
Sandon JMI School, Buntingford

Colours

Blue is a royal waterfall,
Red is a crackling ruby fire,
Yellow is a sparkling sun,
Green is the aqua waving grass,
Orange is a fire breathing dragon,
White is the icy snow,
Brown is a tan bird,
Pink is the cerise rose,
Purple is the smooth bluebell.

Paige Strong (7)
Sandon JMI School, Buntingford

Colours

Purple is the bright, full play hut.
Red is the colour of a clown's nose.
Orange is a lovely fruit.
Yellow is the colour of the bright sun.
Green is a bouncy ball.
Blue is a lively lake.
Brown is the sloppy mud.
Black is the dirty coal we put in the fire.
White is the soft snow.

Luke Geaves (8)
Sandon JMI School, Buntingford

Colours

Red is the beautiful, shiny rose.
Orange is a soft, smooth sofa.
Green is the long, smooth grass.
Pink is a smooth, long door.
Brown is the long tree trunk.
Yellow is the bright sunshine.

Grace Gumble (8)
Sandon JMI School, Buntingford

Stones, Crystals And Rubies

Blue is an icy, blue crystal
Black as a jet-black stone
Green as an aqua-green crystal
White as a snowy-white stone
Brown as a sandy-brown stone
Red as a fiery-red ruby.

Hal Jones (8)
Sandon JMI School, Buntingford

Food

Flour is the sparkling snow,
Spaghetti is a wiggly worm,
Egg is a yellow sun,
Apple is the setting red sun,
Banana is a smoky moon,
An orange is a bouncy ball,
A chocolate is a muddy hole,
Strawberry is a pot of pink paint.

Hannah Stout (9)
Sandon JMI School, Buntingford

Colours

Blue is an icy pond.
Red is a spitting fire.
Yellow is a golden sun.
White is deep snow.
Pink is a shocking flower.
Green is the swishing grass.

Jake Long (8)
Sandon JMI School, Buntingford

Colours

Red is the colour of the best team - Arsenal
Blue is the colour of my pencil
White is part of the colour of our Union Jack
Beige is the colour of lovely chocolate
Yellow is the colour of banana
Purple is a bunch of juicy grapes.

Connor D'Arcy (8)
Sandon JMI School, Buntingford

Colours

Yellow is a golden ring.
Red is the scales of a smoky dragon.
Orange is the colour of flaming fire.
Brown is the colour of rough bark on a tree.
White is the colour of soft snow.
Purple is the colour of bright foxgloves.
Blue is the colour of a salty sea.
Green is the colour of the damp Amazon rainforest.

James Tucker (9)
Sandon JMI School, Buntingford

Plants

Red is a juicy, plump, deep red tomato.
Burgundy is a beautiful leaf scattered on the ground in autumn.
Green is a glistening, delicate stalk.
Pink is an elegant tulip.
Yellow is a fluffy, golden dandelion.
Orange is a delicate marigold.
Red is a precious poppy.
White is a beautiful snowdrop.

Amelia White (8)
Sandon JMI School, Buntingford

Faces

Eyelids blink quickly
Eyes are colourful and shiny
Ears are for hearing interesting words people say
Noses detect wonderful smells
Lips are for pushing out words
Teeth are glistening crystal-white
Faces tell everything.

Danielle Moon (7)
Sandon JMI School, Buntingford

Colours

Blue is a sky thundering on the roof tops.
Red is a pool of bubbly hot lava.
Black is a very deep part of the sea.
Cerise is my sister's bedroom wall.
Brown is a soft, fluffy bear.

Josh Volpe (8)
Sandon JMI School, Buntingford

Colours

Red is the boiling lava gushing down.
Yellow is the gold in the sun.
Green is a pair of smelly socks.
Blue is the sparkling ocean.
Black is the dark night.

Matthew Tucker (8)
Sandon JMI School, Buntingford

Colours

Red is the skin of a ripe tomato.
Green is a cheese and onion Pringle tin.
Blue is a thunderous waterfall.
Black is the side of a jumbo jet.
Yellow is spicy mustard.
Orange is a comfortable sofa.
White is the snow on my garden.
Pink is a tub of strawberry ice cream.

Robert Potts (8)
Sandon JMI School, Buntingford

Colours

Brown is the bark of a rough tree.
White is the icy snow.
Red is a racing sports car.
Black is a starry night.
Orange is a juicy fruit.
Pink is our smooth skin.
Blue is the high sky.

Faye Piggott (7)
Sandon JMI School, Buntingford

Colours

Yellow is a golden sun.
Green is sparkling, waving grass.
White is light, lovely snow.
Red is a ruby-red rose.
Blue is the salty sea.
Pink is a snorting pig.

Philippa Watkins (7)
Sandon JMI School, Buntingford

Colours

Yellow is as gold as the sun.
Brown is as dark as chocolate.
Black is a stormy, dark sky.
Red is shocking like a ghost.
Green is the sparkling grass.
Mauve is as beautiful as the glass.
Blue is the calm sea.

Kristie Childs (8)
Sandon JMI School, Buntingford

Colours

Blue is a sparkling sports car.
Red is a football shirt.
Silver is a massive stadium.
Black is a furry dog.
Green is a small tortoise.
Brown is an Olympic runner.
Gold is a scaly fish.
Lavender is a petalled flower.
Pink is a dragon's tongue.
White is a big snowball.
Orange is a singing bird.
Multicoloured is a bit of everything.

Matthew Stout (8)
Sandon JMI School, Buntingford

Colours

Gold is a glittering, golden light paint.
Green is a light, big, fat frog.
Yellow is a sparkling lemon.
Red is a fat, hungry dragon.
Blue is a light, big swimming pool.
Black is a firing jet.
Brown is a big wall.
Purple is a tiny doll.

Daniel Morris (7)
Sandon JMI School, Buntingford

Snake Haiku

Slithering smoothly,
Its long black body moving,
Hungry hissing snake.

Andrew Marwick (9)
Shapinsay Primary School, Orkney

Dragon

D eafening, loud and
R ough, scaly, red and green, shiny white spikes
A lways flies high in the sky with big wings.
G igantic and crafty, fast
O n top of the world.
N ot sweet and cuddly but fierce and terrifying,
   horrible and alert.

Gail Zawadski (8)
Shapinsay Primary School, Orkney

Rabbits

R abbits are soft and cute
A mazing creatures
B ouncing all day long, nearly touching the sky
B eautiful bunny as warm as can be
I t munches juicy orange carrots
T heir tails are fluffy and soft.

Rachel Muir (8)
Shapinsay Primary School, Orkney

Pokémon

P owerful and
O utstanding attacks
K ept in tiny Pokéballs
É xciting and enjoyable games
M unching Pokéblocks
O ften helpful and very funny
N ice and cute.

Jake Houston (8)
Shapinsay Primary School, Orkney

Young Writers - Playground Poets Pens Down

Griffin

G reat, scaly, monstrous creature
R eally sly, slender and sneaky
I ncredibly large, violent
F ierce, sharp claws
F righteningly evil
I maginative animal
N asty six limbed beast.

Emily Farquharson (11)
Shapinsay Primary School, Orkney

My Counting Poem

One white whale waving warily
Two tapping tigers taking tables
Three thinking thrushes thought thoroughly
Four fat fish feeling funny
Five flamingos flying fish
Six slow slugs sitting scarily
Seven snails singing slowly
Eight echoing elephants emptying eggs
Nine napping newts knitting nicely
Ten typing turtles tipping trash.

Taylor Wall (9)
Siddington CE Primary School, Siddington

Limerick

The school trip was a special occasion
But we never reached our destination
The school bus broke down
In the middle of town
So we all rushed along to the station.

Sam Burgess (10)
Siddington CE Primary School, Siddington

Counting Poem

One white whale watching the wasp.
Two trembling tigers tingling the triangle.
Three thick thrushes thinking thoroughly.
Four fighting flamingos feeling funny.
Five frightened fish firmly fighting.
Six singing snails sizzling sausages.
Seven slimy snakes scaring slugs.
Eight eating elephants eating enormous eggs.
Nine nice newts nicking nibbles.
Ten teaching tortoises teaching teachers time.

Sapphire Rogers (10)
Siddington CE Primary School, Siddington

Counting Poem

One white wombat worried a weak worm
Two trembling tortoises took two tickets to tenpin bowling
Three blind mice went running through the garage
Four freaky fish swam from France
Five frogs jumped through the pond.

Emma Walker (9)
Siddington CE Primary School, Siddington

The Knight

(Inspired by 'The Highwayman' by Alfred Noyes)

The sky is a flowering blossom among the dusky sky,
The mountain is a fiery gleam tossed upon the clouds,
The rainbow is a stream of colours upon the dull air,
And the knight came patrolling, patrolling, patrolling,
The knight came patrolling up to the old castle door.

Oberon Rogers (10)
Siddington CE Primary School, Siddington

The Highwayman
(Inspired by 'The Highwayman' by Alfred Noyes)

The highwayman only comes out at night.
People walking, their bodies get such a fright.
From the jewelled, starry night, or like travelling through space.
Scaring, scaring, scaring every single person who goes near him.
But watch, he goes at his own pace.
The brown horse is speeding.
The highwayman is pleading.
You can never see him at day.
Riding, riding, riding to the pub
Trying to find his way.
He has a pair of leather boots up to his thigh.
Underneath the jewelled sky.
When he enters the bar, there is silence.
Drinking, drinking, drinking what is put in front of him
But when he starts there is violence.

Daniella Keen (10)
Siddington CE Primary School, Siddington

The Window Incident

Through the window goes the ball, rolling round the hall
Here comes the teacher, he is such a screecher,
Here comes the head, take a runner,
The head is like a mad machine gunner,
He has his cane, he is coming this way,
I have to use my brain,
I've got it, I'll hide in the bin . . .
Very smelly . . . not good for your belly,
But away from the head . . . I'm safe!

Harry Tainton (10)
Westbury-on-Trym CE Primary School, Bristol

Cool Queen

I read it in a book one day,
I saw it in a paper,
The Queen was going to come and stay -
Travelling in her hotring racer!

She knocked on the door that day
'Hello,' I said, 'come in.
I would love to say how privileged
We are that you're here!'
'It'll be wicked!' she replied,
'Cool! Amazing!' she exclaimed.
What was this, 'a cool queen' in my house?
I thought she'd be posh - like Ratty, my pet mouse!
'So, wazz up?' she asked, doing a peace sign.
'I've brought some cool tunes along -
R 'n' B rhymes!'

Charlotte Vincent (11)
Westbury-on-Trym CE Primary School, Bristol

Flying

Easily soaring through the sky.
Watching as the days go by.
Flying high in the sky.
Do you wish you could fly?
My wings are pretty,
My wings are beautiful,
Not very dull.
Who do you think I am?
Am I a bird, have you heard?
You guessed right,
I am a bird.

Danielle Johns (8)
Westbury-on-Trym CE Primary School, Bristol

Trains

We went to get a train to go away,
To another place,
Somewhere quiet.
I wait for a second,
I wait for a minute,
I wait for an hour
And then I heard a *chu chu!*

It began moving,
Faster and faster,
And then the wheels said *chig chig chigidig*
When we were travelling,
The wheels went slower
And then I heard, creak!

Now it was time to go home,
We got off the train
And I heard the train say *chu chu!*
I heard myself saying,
'That was a good ride.'

Emier Villanueva (10)
Westbury-on-Trym CE Primary School, Bristol

My Cat

My cat licks and flicks
My cat walks and talks
My cat bites and fights
My cat dives and jives
My cat twirls and whirls
What a funny cat I have!

Chloe Paddock (8)
Westbury-on-Trym CE Primary School, Bristol

My Headteacher Is An Alien And He's Trying To Vaporise Me!

It started on parent evening,
Dad went in to talk,
He left me in the cloakroom,
So I went out for a walk,
I decided to return home,
(The school was painted pink)
I got back just in time for tea,
And watched 'The Weakest Link'.
Tea I learnt, was moussaka,
It made my stomach churn,
Mum asked me where Dad was,
He never did return,
Then it killed my neighbour,
Then the rest of my family,
I wonder if it'll ever stop,
Until it has killed me.
Now it's following me in school,
From my classroom to the bathroom wall,
Eventually I killed it,
Inside the swimming pool,
Its body was made mainly from salt,
The rest from milk and honey
And also custard and mustard,
It's really rather funny.

Daniel Squire (11)
Westbury-on-Trym CE Primary School, Bristol

Fantasy

Fairy with a wand that glitters
With her wings away she flitters
Pirate with a glinting knife
Don't go too close, you'll lose your life!

Wicked witch with poison brew
She is planning to kill you!
Alien spaceship in the sky
See the planets passing by.

I can be a pretty fairy
Or a pirate that is scary!
Wicked witch with poison brew
Or an alien that waves to you!

Now, you might think that that's a strain
But maybe you should think again
Leave all the boring things behind
And dream a fantasy in your mind.

Mathilda Forrester (9)
Westbury-on-Trym CE Primary School, Bristol

Monkeys

See a monkey swinging on a tree.
See a monkey wave at you and me.
See a monkey doing a dance.
See a monkey trying to trance.
Hear a monkey rustling in a tree.
Hear a monkey scratching his knee.
Hear a monkey eating his lunch.
Hear a monkey crunch, crunch, crunch.

Megan Dymmock-Morgan (7)
Westbury-on-Trym CE Primary School, Bristol

Let Them Be A Child Again

Let them spend a day in our shoes!
Let them be a child again
Because I think they might have forgot
What it's like to be bossed around by such a bossy lot,
Not allowed to play
Because you have to go to school every day
And then when, in two special days
When you get a break
You have to tidy your bedroom
Which we absolutely *hate!*

Let them go to bed early,
Lights off straight away,
When that could be the perfect time,
The perfect time to play!

Let them have Brussels sprouts
Yuck, yuck, yuck, yuck!
Because without a doubt
They're just a load of muck!

But now you must stop
And think they were once actually us,
So maybe they're taking their turn,
Their turn to be boss
So one day, not so far away
We'll be them
And *we'll* think children are mayhem!

Carys Gilbert (8)
Westbury-on-Trym CE Primary School, Bristol

The Day Gran And Grandad Visited

When I heard Gran and Grandad were coming
It was really quite a shock.
They live in Canada you see,
So they do not come a lot.

They don't act like old wrinklies,
They can actually be quite fun.
They are not from my mum's side,
So my father is their son.

Grandma says how small things are
Like houses, trees and cars.
Grandad doesn't say a lot
Except when he's in bars.

My father calls them Mum and Dad
Which sometimes sounds quite strange,
Because when their son is not around
They both act half my age!

Gran often rides the floor broom
Mom says, she's humane,
I wish I could go up to her
And say, 'Gran, you are insane!'

We said goodbye, their time to go,
I really thought I'd miss them,
Then reality struck down,
I knew I had to kiss them!

Demi Orchard (11)
Westbury-on-Trym CE Primary School, Bristol

Rat

Jumps
Onto the shelf
Leaps
And falls out the other end
Lands
On the others
Creeps
Up the tube
Sees
The sunlight streaming in
Eats
Everything it can
Lies
On the floor
Wakes
All tired and sleepy
Begs
For grapes to eat
Goes
To play with the others
After
A run around
Until
The lights go out
Quiet
All around
Wait
Until some noise
Awake
Won't go to sleep
A day
Of being a rat.

Jenny Seaborne (10)
Westbury-on-Trym CE Primary School, Bristol

Dolphins

Dolphins jump, dolphins thump
Dolphins are blue, dolphins flow in the deep blue sea.
They flutter, they flick
See the dolphin kick and flick.
But when I went to see the aquarium I saw . . .
A dolphin but there was something wrong about it.
It wasn't blue, it wasn't fluttering and flickering
It wasn't kicking.
It was just lying there doing nothing
And it was grey.
I thought it might be a shark . . . but I knew it wasn't.
I asked the aquarium owner and he said it was a dolphin.
I love dolphins, do you?

Sophie Haydon (7)
Westbury-on-Trym CE Primary School, Bristol

My Day

First it's breakfast, then I'll go and pack,
Off to school with my rucksack on my back,
First lesson of the day, art - hooray!
Assembly's next, then it's break,
My yummy snack is a slice of cake.
Maths then lunch, I've got an apple to crunch!
In the afternoon we read then do PE,
Science is next, oh boy - yippee!
At the end of the day, Mum picks me up to say,
'Hello darling, did you have a nice day?'
I skip home from school, to get my tea in my tum,
I'll watch a bit of telly, then a cuddle from Mum,
I'm quite tired now, I think I'll go to bed,
Under the covers and cuddle my ted.
That was my day.

Katy Farmer (10)
Westbury-on-Trym CE Primary School, Bristol

Oh I Wish I Had Some Friends

Wandering around the playground
Sad as ever I could be
Children play I see.

I wish I had some friends
No more, no less
I don't care if they're fat or small
Or thin or tall.

'Jane, Jane, can I play?'
'No, no, you're too slow.'
Oh how sad I am
Really I am,
Oh I wish I had some friends.

Nisha Dave (8)
Westbury-on-Trym CE Primary School, Bristol

Friends!

When you're feeling drowsy,
When something's messing up your head,
A friend is always there to help
So you feel happy instead!

When your friend is hurt,
When your friend is sad,
You are always there to help
So they don't feel bad!

When you're both unhappy,
When you're both upset,
You can cheer each other up
So that you won't fret!

Bláithín Garrad (8)
Westbury-on-Trym CE Primary School, Bristol

Tigers

The tiger's eyes, dark and fierce
Pounces on its prey.
Shreds its food to little bits
And then goes out to play.
Do you think you'll get stopped by a tiger?

Jack Hooper (8)
Westbury-on-Trym CE Primary School, Bristol

Bro

Bro is a mud pit
A please play with me kitten,
A run and catch me leopard,
A goose feather duvet,
But sometimes he's a needle in the neck,
A piece of chewing gum in my hair,
A pool of bleach,
A polluted world.

Jade Legge (11)
Ystruth Primary School, Blaina

Roxi

Roxi is a barrel of growls,
A snarl at the window,
A bone carrier,
A wagging tail at dinner time,
A vending machine for her puppies.

Abbie James (10)
Ystruth Primary School, Blaina

Dad

Dad is a real-life Homer Simpson.
A bone-crunching, meat-munching machine.
A fast spinning waltzer ride.
A cracked leg of a chair.

But sometimes he's a blaring trumpet.
An angry referee.
A padlock on a wallet.
Leave me.

Corey Williams (10)
Ystruth Primary School, Blaina

Fish

Fish is an Olympic swimmer
A 100% treat gobbler
A swirl in a bowl
Luscious liquorice throat sweet

But sometimes he's a . . .
Big black bully
A bucket of coal
An evacuee without a ration!

Tanith Parfitt (10)
Ystruth Primary School, Blaina

My Dog

Soft like bird feathers.
He's a wild howl in the night,
A bolt of lightning,
A gold medal jumper,
He's a squeak, squeak ball-chasing freak.

Beckie Price (11)
Ystruth Primary School, Blaina

Gizzy

Gizzy is a white, fluffy cloud,
A fast, miniature cheetah, she is a play with me ball,
She is a tickle my tummy, she is a wild run around the house,
Gizzy is a climb up the curtains,
But sometimes she is a scram in the face,
She is a bite you in the hand, a racing car without any petrol,
She is a rule breaking outlaw.

Gemma Ball (11)
Ystruth Primary School, Blaina

A Waterfall

A waterfall splashes.
It bubbles like a fish.
It hisses like a snake.
It swirls like a tornado.
It splatters like paint.
It bounces like a jack-in-the-box.

Daniel Wall (11)
Ystruth Primary School, Blaina

Dad

Dad is a remote control, an iron bar,
A Strongbow gulper,
A belly laugh, a sweet and sour sauce.
Dad is a peddle fast down the hill.
But sometimes he's a stamping foot,
A booking traffic warden, a black, rainy cloud,
A straight fishing line,
A hammer-hit finger.

Adam Hughes (10)
Ystruth Primary School, Blaina

Mam

Mam is a bottle of bleach,
A powerful Hoover, karate kid window cleaner,
Dustpan and brush, one thousand tool handyman,
Fix me quick motorbike,
But sometimes she's . . .
A broken cash machine, a security guard on duty,
A screech of brakes, a get off the computer!

Rhys Watkins (11)
Ystruth Primary School, Blaina

A Waterfall Feature

A waterfall slaps like thunder,
It swirls like ice cream,
It jingles like bells,
It springs with action,
It giggles like a pantomime,
It bubbles like a hot bath.

Demi Cooper (11)
Ystruth Primary School, Blaina

Pepsi Is . . .

Pepsi is . . .
A run around till I'm dizzy,
A gravity resistance,
A let's have some fun tail wagger,
A bouncy ball,
A dynamo,
A cuddly teddy bear.

Aimee Smith-Holden (10)
Ystruth Primary School, Blaina

Dad

Dad is 450 megabytes of computer,
An open tool box,
A Xbox time bandit,
A million decibel scream,
A dripping ice cream sundae.

But sometimes he's . . .
A don't do that,
A referee with a whistle,
A stretched elastic band,
A wild tiger,
A spilt glass of milk.

Ieuan Ward (11)
Ystruth Primary School, Blaina